TENNIS LOVE

ILLUSTRATIONS BY

Charles M. Schulz

TENNIS LOVE

A PARENTS' GUIDE
TO THE SPORT

Billie Jean King
and Greg Hoffman

Macmillan Publishing Co., Inc.

NEW YORK

Macmillan Publishing Co., Inc.
866 Third Avenue, New York, N.Y. 10022
Collier Macmillan Canada, Ltd.

Library of Congress Cataloging in Publication Data
King, Billie Jean.   /   Tennis love.
1. Tennis.   /   2. Tennis—Psychological aspects.
I. Hoffman, Greg, 1946–   joint author.   /   II. Title.
GV995.K496   /   796.34'22   /   77-25864
ISBN 0-02-563210-8

First Printing 1978
Printed in the United States of America

Excerpt reprinted by permission, from Sports Psyching,
by Thomas Tutko, Ph.D., and Umberto Tosi, © *1976,*
published by J.P. Tarcher, Inc., 9110 Sunset Boulevard,
Los Angeles, California 90069, $6.95.

Exercise illustrations by Mike Dowdall.

To parents with the patience and understanding of

BILL AND BETTY MOFFITT,

and to children with the future of

JASON MICHAEL HOFFMAN.

Contents

TENNIS LOVE

Introduction: Why Tennis?

When the idea of writing a tennis book for parents was first presented to me, I was extremely hesitant. The notion of telling parents how to teach their children the game of tennis just wasn't appealing. In fact, my initial reaction was that the subject could be nicely handled by one simple word: "Don't."

Tennis is a high-technique sport and one that the average parent is probably not equipped to teach. There are, I admit, a few exceptions. I am well aware that Chris Evert, for example, is a product of her father's instruction, and she hasn't fared too badly. But it's important to remember that her father, Jimmy Evert, had been teaching tennis for almost ten years before Chris was even born.

Most parents don't have a decade of teaching experience behind them, and quite often their children are their first, last, and only pupils. Despite every good intention in the world, mothers or fathers who assume the role of tennis instructor will probably be doing their children more harm than good.

After all, teaching practically any skill that requires a certain amount of physical dexterity and coordination can be a difficult and frustrating experience. If the instructor and student are members of the same family, and especially if they are parent and child, those frustrations are often compounded. There are more than enough normal tensions in everyday family life, so why take the chance of adding more, especially in the area of family recreation. I believe anything that might possibly diminish the enjoyment of a family playing together should be avoided like the plague.

All of which brings us back to tennis, a sport that is currently enjoying a phenomenal surge of popularity and is attracting new converts like a smooth-talking evangelist.

Eighty million people may sit in their living rooms to *watch* the Super Bowl on television, but almost half that number actually go out and *play* tennis.

A recent survey predicts that within a few years over thirty million households in the United States will have at least one tennis player in residence, and we can safely assume that a fair percentage of those households will be made up of entire families who have taken up racquets. Even now, a casual expedition to the local courts will confirm that the number of tennis families is on the upswing.

But what combination of circumstances has caused that tradition-ridden, staid, elitist, country-club pastime to suddenly sweep the country like an unchecked flu epidemic almost a full century after it was introduced? There are, of course, several reasons. In my opinion the grass-roots infatuation with tennis began in 1968. Prior to that watershed year, tennis had always been basically an amateur sport, at least on the surface. Without going into the hypocrisy and under-the-table money exchanges that tennis' strict code of amateurism engendered, suffice it to say that in 1968 it became officially acceptable to earn a living playing tennis.

That long overdue turn of events somehow transformed tennis from a diversion for the idle rich into a legitimate sport

4

in the eyes of the public. Everyone, from factory worker to corporate president, can relate to money and sports, especially today when a professional athlete's financial statement gets almost as much ink as his batting average or free-throw percentage.

Not surprisingly, the exposure tennis began to receive rose in direct proportion to the amount of money being offered by the various tournaments. Gradually, the attention began to have an effect, the fruits of which we are now experiencing.

But if the exposure generated by open tennis brought the sport to the attention of the masses, it is an emerging national concern with physical fitness and good health that has encouraged many people to take up the game. As a result, tennis suddenly became *the* sport of the seventies. But it is more than that. Much more. It is also the perfect family sport because it knows no sex or age barriers. With the possible exception of the family pet, anyone can play. (Actually, there is at least one athletically inclined canine whose tennis exploits have been well documented.) And, since it accommodates all skill levels,

tennis offers families the unique opportunity to share a common athletic activity. Parents, children, and even grandparents can get together for a few hours of feeling good and having fun with tennis—and that's fantastic.

With all due respect to George Blanda, it is difficult to imagine Grandma and Grandpa running around on a football field, a basketball court, or a baseball diamond, but they can and do play tennis without causing traffic jams or attracting curious stares. Long after the family elders have put their skis in permanent storage and hung up their basketball sneakers for the last·time, they can still grab a tennis racquet and try to knock the fuzz off the ball.

The active senior citizens are living proof that tennis can provide a lifetime of enjoyment and exercise. Many of the children who are taking up the game today will still be playing fifty, sixty, even seventy years from now. Many other children, though, will reject tennis somewhere along the line. Perhaps they'll decide, after being exposed to the game, that it just isn't the sport for them and they'll move on to something else. Or maybe they won't feel comfortable playing any sport. That's fine because nowhere is it written that children have to play tennis, or any other sport for that matter.

But it's something else entirely when an *unnecessary* outside influence causes a child to abandon tennis—like an overbearing parent who pushes too hard or expects too much, for instance.

Thinking about all of this finally brought me to the realization that a book about the parent-child-tennis triangle might not be such a bad idea after all, that, in fact, it would be an important and extremely beneficial book.

Once my enthusiasm for the project had been ignited, the next step was to decide on a format. Obviously, because of my belief that parents should generally avoid teaching their children, an instruction manual would be inappropriate. Besides, there are already a number of excellent ones available that expertly demonstrate the mechanics of the game.

I also didn't want to do a "How-to-make-your-child-a-tennis-champ"–type book. I couldn't have written that one even if I'd wanted to. I don't think anyone can. It's definitely one thing that cannot be broken down into a formula; it is the result of something inside a person and very, very few individuals have it. Pure physical skill isn't quite enough. There are thousands of tennis players who have picture-perfect strokes but who will never rise to the top because they lack that certain internal intangible. Call it determination, drive, will, desire, or whatever, but call it rare. A technically superb player who doesn't have it is like a musician who is able to duplicate flawlessly the notes of a master, but can't put an original melody together to save his life.

So rather than do a book that tells parents how to teach their children or how to mold them into future champions, I decided to prepare a parents' *guide* to tennis.

Though the practical aspects of the game are by no means ignored—discussions concerning equipment, court etiquette, strategy, etc., are included—the primary emphasis is on how to *help* your children rather than on how to teach them: How to help them obtain proper instruction in the fundamentals; how to help them deal with competition; and, generally, how to help them get the most out of their involvement with tennis. Most importantly, however, I hope this book will show parents how to help their children have *fun* with tennis. After all, having fun is what tennis, or any sport, is all about. At least that's what it *should* be all about. If it's not, something is drastically wrong.

Though I'm neither a parent nor a psychologist, I believe that much of what I have so far seen and experienced during my years in tennis will enable me to provide you with an outline for enhancing your child's enjoyment of the game. All I can unconditionally guarantee, however, is that there are no easy, 100 percent foolproof answers. I know because I've looked for them.

I

The Importance of

Playing Sports

Since the need to play is a basic element of the human condition, it is only natural for a strong sports consciousness to become a deeply interwoven part of the fabric of our society.

Sports, of course, are those various physical activities which we indulge in for pleasure and to satisfy our need to play. Though accurate, that particular definition of sports is somewhat simplistic. It says nothing, for instance, about the considerable influence sports has on many of our lives.

If you think that is an exaggeration, just take a look around. Consider, for example, the fact that more and more athletes are rivaling movie stars in terms of mass popularity. Then there are the mind-boggling numbers that are associated with sports: college football games occasionally put 100,000 people in seats; the three commercial television networks in this country scramble all over each other for the chance to shell out over $85 million for the right to broadcast the Olympic Games; and forty million Americans play tennis.

The latter number is indicative of an important and healthy trend: the unprecedented growth of participation in sports. A substantial portion of that growth is the increasingly active role the female segment of the population is now taking in sports. No longer are athletics primarily a male preserve.

Playing sports is good for everybody, so it is gratifying that we are finally getting to the point where everybody *can* participate. For far too long girls and women were relegated to the sidelines, but now they can play without suffering the humiliation of being branded with a figurative scarlet *A* (for athlete). As one measure of the increased female participation in at least one sport, there are more women than men taking up tennis.

One hopes that the increased participation and involvement in athletics by members of both sexes will continue. Fortunately, many schools are doing their part to insure that it will by instructing very young children on the importance of sports.

So there is little doubt that sports play a major role in our lives. Equally important, however, is the fact that they actually *relate* to life on several different levels. Because of that relationship, we are learning that early athletic experiences can greatly affect a child's emotional and psychological growth. That is the view currently being expressed by many psychologists, and it is one with which I find myself in complete agreement.

Though the bottom line of sports is that it is a source of relaxation and enjoyment, on a more philosophical level it can teach us to deal with adversity in a positive manner. It can also show us the value of learning to laugh at ourselves when things don't go exactly our way, a not infrequent occurrence in practically any athletic endeavor. That may sound a little strange, but it's no accident that many professional athletes have highly developed senses of humor. Without them, they couldn't survive. The ability to laugh at yourself is almost a requirement for a successful career in athletics.

On a more practical level, sports gives us—adults and children alike—a legitimate, socially acceptable means of periodically releasing our pent-up tensions and aggressions. We all have them, and as any parent will testify, children seem to possess more than their fair share. But many psychologists believe that children who learn to channel these natural aggressions in a constructive way—say through the atmosphere of structured freedom offered by sports in general and tennis in particular—often have a head start toward building a strong emotional foundation.

Though obviously preferable to temper tantrums or sibling

warfare in the kitchen, sports is by no means the ultimate kiddie tranquilizer. It is helpful, but not foolproof. And although the importance of playing sports cannot be overestimated, parents should be aware that sports' potential to traumatize is ever present. That decidedly negative aspect of sports is due to the fact that athletic performances are both visible and measurable. Successes are laid out for everyone to see, but so are the failures.

For illustrative purposes, consider the case of a ten-year-old halfback on an organized football team who fumbles the ball away on an important play. The fumble cannot be kept a secret. The player's coaches, teammates, opponents, and parents all know it has occurred, and they will all react to it in

some way. Obviously, the player knows he has fumbled and that knowledge will have an effect on him. But it needn't be a traumatic one. If he has been taught that everyone makes mistakes from time to time and that such mistakes are not the end of the world, he will be fine. On the other hand, if a zealous coach or parent has convinced him that fumbling or dropping a pass is inexcusable because it adversely affects the entire team, the unfortunate player stands an excellent chance of becoming paralyzed by the fear of falling on his face. It's no wonder that a bad athletic experience can cause a kid to fold like a napkin.

In the past, it has been baseball and football youth programs that have drawn the most fire for putting kids under potentially damaging pressures, but no sport is truly immune from that charge. I've certainly seen more than enough young tennis casualties over the years and each and every one makes me cringe.

Life is not perfect and neither is sports. But with a little bit of parental patience, guidance, and common sense every child should be able to play without fear, guilt, or pressure.

They are entitled to nothing less.

2

A Case in Point:

Love at First Swipe

Looking back, I can say that I was very lucky when I was a child. My parents somehow managed to hit all the right notes during my early development as an athlete.

Long before I had ever heard of tennis, much less played it, I had decided that I wanted a career in sports. Of course at the time I was completely unaware that the odds were heavily stacked against me. I'm not entirely sure I would have been discouraged if I had known, but I have to give my parents a lot of credit for not telling me that I was being unrealistic and that I'd be better off setting my sights on a career as a housewife instead. I'm sure that's what they wanted, though, which makes their restraint all the more remarkable.

Not many girls growing up in the fifties planned to devote their lives to sports, so I guess I was a little bit different.

When I was only four or five, I used to drag my father outside to play catch with me, and when we weren't doing that he was usually timing my endless series of 50-yard dashes up and down the street in front of our house in Long Beach, California.

Actually, it seldom required much effort to get my father to come out and play because he shared my love of sports. Or

14

should I say that I shared his love of sports? Either way, he also possessed a surplus of that valuable commodity known as patience, which was indeed fortunate. For both of us.

Then a few years later, when I was ten, I joined a girls' fifteen-and-under softball team that had been organized by the Long Beach Recreation Department. I was the youngest player on the team, but the countless number of hours playing catch with my father had polished my skills enough to enable me to play a credible second base. Later in the season I was moved over to third base, and then finally to shortstop.

I clearly remember that we had to cut our family vacation trip to the mountains short that summer so I would be home in time to play in the City Championship softball game. I could hardly contain my excitement when my team won even though I already knew that baseball was not the sport to accommodate my dream of becoming a professional athlete.

I had learned that sad fact the previous Mother's Day, when my father took me to a Pacific Coast League baseball game between the Hollywood Stars and the Los Angeles Angels. I was so enthralled with the action that it wasn't until sometime around the fifth inning that I realized there were no women on the field. Not even one! That was really a crushing blow. And, as if that particular discovery wasn't bad enough, my mother had been making threatening noises about my football and basketball activities as well. We had some terrific neighborhood games, and I had developed into a pretty fair halfback and an accurate outside shooter. Then, like millions of other active ten-year-old girls, I was told that running the fly pattern, sliding into home, and shooting jumpshots fell a bit short of acceptable "ladylike" behavior. I couldn't believe that something that was so much fun was "wrong" just because I happened to be a girl. Somehow it didn't seem fair, and I was beginning to wonder if I'd ever find a sport that would give me a career *and* be acceptable to my mother.

Then, with exquisitely perfect timing, I got my first taste of the game that would dominate my life. Strange as it seems, I had never heard of tennis until just a few months before my eleventh birthday. That's when a friend of mine, who'd learned the game while she was living in New York, dropped by and suggested we play.

"Sure thing," I said, "but what's tennis?"

I soon found out. My friend found a spare racquet for me, and we walked over to the local courts. And we played tennis. She did, anyway. I mainly ran around chasing balls I'd missed. I didn't know the first thing about scoring or the basics of the game, but I immediately decided that tennis was the sport for me; and I do mean immediately. Despite my often frustrating attempts to make contact with the ball, I felt an exhilaration and sense of absolute freedom that's impossible to describe.

Tennis was a challenge, of course, and that appealed to me. But the fact that it combined the elements of movement

and total involvement is what really cemented my affection for the game. When I was on that court running and swinging at the ball I felt like I was dancing on a cloud, and I never wanted to stop.

A lot of years have passed since then, but I can honestly say that today I feel exactly the same way I did on that long ago afternoon in Long Beach when I hit a tennis ball for the first time.

Discovering tennis was the greatest thing that ever happened to me.

3

Tennis and Children:

Young Love

Without trying to sound overly mystic, I would have to say that my involvement with tennis seems almost predestined. It would not be farfetched to suggest that the game chose me as surely as I chose the game.

For one thing, my introduction to tennis came precisely at that time in my life when I was looking for something to replace the sports I loved but that had suddenly become taboo. Then there was the casual, out-of-the-blue manner in which I was exposed to the game. One day tennis just didn't exist in my world, and the next it *was* my world.

Neither of my parents played tennis. As a matter of fact, I wasn't able to talk my dad into picking up a racquet until 1968, nearly fifteen years after I started playing. When the tennis establishment officially recognized the pro element, he finally consented to give it a try. Until then, he considered tennis to be a pastime for the country-club set, a view shared by many people.

That image, of course, has changed considerably in recent years. The great majority of youngsters flocking to tennis courts today are doing so because of a prior exposure to the

18

game, most likely either by television or by their parents.

As an example of the latter, I know one couple who introduced their son to tennis well before he reached his first birthday. Whenever they went out to play, the couple would hang the baby's portable car seat, with the infant firmly strapped therein, on the chain link fence which enclosed the court. Apparently believing that it was totally natural to be hung up in that manner, the child offered no protest. In fact, he rather enjoyed it. The parents' ingenuity also saved a fortune in babysitting fees, so things worked out all the way around.

Before long, however, the child outgrew his unique ringside seat. No problem. He became the family's official ball boy, a position he initially filled with enthusiasm if not grace. He was thrilled by his contribution to the proceeding, and as time went on, he became highly competent in the performance of his duties. Then, just about the time he began to tire of chasing the balls, his parents presented him with a racquet. They lost a ball boy, but gained a tennis player.

Well, that's one way of doing it, but regardless of the route that brings a child to tennis, the trip should be worthwhile. Why? It's very simple really. There are few sports more ideally suited to children than good ol' tennis.

I have already discussed a few of the reasons why it is a terrific family sport, but there are a number of additional factors that make tennis an especially great activity for children.

It is neither excessively time-consuming nor prohibitively expensive. Sure, you can spend a small fortune on equipment, clothing, and gadgets if you want, but the basic necessities can be had without having to mortgage your home.

Also, tennis is a non-violent, non-contact sport, which is an important consideration for parents who are rightfully concerned with the physical well-being of the young athletes in

19

the family. I don't mean to imply that it is completely risk-free. Few sports are. Still, the chances of a child being injured on a tennis court are not nearly as great as they are in many other sports. And the possibility of a child suffering a serious, or fatal, tennis injury are practically non-existent.

Since it is a technique sport, tennis offers the child not blessed with an overabundance of natural athletic ability the opportunity to excel in an athletic endeavor. Chris Evert, for example, is not your basic, raw-talent athlete, but she has established herself as one of the best tennis players of all time. Her tennis skills and successes, both of which are impressive, are the result of a tremendous amount of hard work, dedication, and a sense of competitiveness that is as solid as a block of granite.

Of course, raw talent doesn't hurt any, but the absence of same does not automatically preempt the chance to play tennis and play it well.

Tennis also differs from many sports in that it does not put a premium on physical size. The small child who is a human doormat on the football field or who has a difficult time trying to put the basketball through the hoop might very well find a home on the tennis court.

Harold Solomon and Rosie Casals immediately come to mind as two rather short professional tennis players who nevertheless stand tall on the court. Each has compensated for a lack of height in totally different but equally effective (for them) ways. Harold wears down his opponents, including those who are much taller and stronger than he, with his unwavering steadiness, while Rosie calls on her quickness and range.

Tracy Austin is yet another impressive player of less than imposing physical size. In early 1977, just two months after she turned fourteen, Tracy was playing on the Virginia Slims Circuit against the top women players in the world—all ninety

pounds of her, and that included the ribbons on her pigtails. She then went on to become the youngest player ever to win a match at Wimbledon, and who can forget her amazing performance at the 1977 U.S. Open where she reached the quarterfinals?

Since tennis doesn't discriminate against the child not blessed with natural athletic talent or substantial size, it has welcomed into its ranks many children who might not have otherwise known the sheer joy of playing sports. It also doesn't discriminate in another area: A lot of those children are female.

Tennis, of course, has always been sexually integrated to a large degree, and in fact, it was a woman named Mary Outerbridge who, in 1874, first brought the sport to these shores. And on the professional level, tennis is one of a tiny handful of sports in which women can earn as much as men.

21

Unfortunately, however, the aspect of sexual integration of tennis has caused the game to become the primary focal point for the male versus female confrontation in sports. I must admit I am partially responsible for that because of the Bobby Riggs match a few years back, but I honestly don't feel the question is all that important. Let's face it, a good man player can beat a good woman player of approximately the same age. Who cares? It doesn't really prove anything.

Maybe someday in the distant future women will be competing with men in tennis as a matter of course, but right now we should try to concentrate on removing the last remnants of the psychological barriers that girls and women must contend with in sports.

Tennis is certainly one sport that's showing the way in that area. There is no specifically "male" or "female" way of playing tennis. Tennis is tennis, period. The fundamentals are exactly the same for men and women and boys and girls. And, as I've said more than once, there hasn't ever been a tennis ball that could tell whether the racquet that struck it was held by a male or female.

One more factor that makes tennis especially well suited for children regardless of sex is that it is a predominantly individual sport. I have played both individual and team sports, and I definitely believe that children should experience both. But I also feel that individual sports, such as tennis, are preferable for younger children.

Team sports do provide plenty of opportunity for a child to learn leadership and cooperation with others, but their basic structure can also lead a child to develop a tendency to pass the buck, to blame others for a poor showing instead of saying, "Hey, maybe I could do better."

Team sports are further burdened with a problem completely foreign to tennis, namely that a large number of people are required for a game. Because of this, age-group participation in team sports may be graphically illustrated by a pyramid. Participation is extremely broad at the base of the pyramid which represents organized youth programs. The narrowing begins at the high school level and continues to shrink when college-age participants are included. The pyramid reaches its apex with professional sports. Basically, what all this means is that only a tiny percentage of youngsters who play Little League baseball, for instance, will find their names on a major league contract. Obviously, the same relative percentages apply to tennis—very few make it to the top—but a tennis player doesn't have to rustle up two dozen people for a game.

Tennis players also have the added advantage of being able to play their sport without regard to the passage of years. On the other hand, the team athlete's playing days usually end well before the age of forty. As a result, ex-ballplayers often seen to fall apart physically unless they stumble onto another outlet.

For precisely that reason, I would personally like to see the school systems promote "lifetime" sports, such as tennis. Children should be thoroughly educated about the benefits of lifetime sports and encouraged to get involved in one or several of them away from school.

If you think I'm trying to ignore the fact that tennis can also be a team sport, let me assure you that is not the case at all. There's the Davis Cup for men and the Wightman Cup and Federation Cup for women, and many high schools and colleges field tennis teams. These competitions, however, are team events only in the sense that they are comprised of several *individual* matches. The World Team Tennis version of the game comes closest to presenting tennis as a true team sport. WTT does it with a unique format in which men and women players have their individual game (not set) victories cumulatively totaled to decide the final outcome of a five-set match. WTT also allows substitutions during the competition, a familiar aspect of the more established team sports.

I haven't forgotten that doubles and mixed doubles, which certainly may be defined as team efforts, are very popular among recreation tennis players. It's just that the basic foundation of tennis has been and always will be primarily an individual endeavor.

Because the emphasis is placed on individual effort, tennis can teach a child discipline and self-reliance while at the same time leaving plenty of room for expressing individuality and creativity. That may sound somewhat contradictory, but it isn't really.

The opportunity to be creative on the court is, in my

opinion, one of tennis' most appealing aspects. The options available to a player during a match are literally endless. Every shot presents a new challenge. Though tennis serves up more variety than a string of Baskin-Robbins franchises, the variables aren't restricted solely to shot-making.

A player must be acutely aware of his or her own strengths and weaknesses and must be able to determine those of the person on the other side of the net quickly and accurately. Everyone's game has an Achilles heel, and the effective player will find his opponent's and try to take advantage of it.

Tennis is a game that requires a tremendous amount of thinking and constant adjustment. Mental agility must be coordinated with physical effort and that particular combination, when successfully blended, can go a long way toward building a child's confidence.

But while children can run around swinging at the ball to their hearts' content, they know they are limited by the dimensions of the court, the height of the net, and the rules of the game. This is what I mean by the "structured freedom" of tennis. Everything must be accomplished within the limits imposed by these restraints. But don't worry, the limitations won't inhibit the young player. On the contrary, they provide children with a very real and necessary sense of security. The rules and regulations tell them just exactly how far they and their opponent may go. Everything is even-steven, and that's definitely one concept every child can relate to with no problem.

And with that, ladies and gentlemen, I rest my case. I think there can be no doubt that tennis and children were made for each other.

4

Tennis Parents:

The Good, the Bad, and

the Obnoxious

I was working out at a tennis club near San Francisco a few months after my November 1976 knee operation when I witnessed a scene that both fascinated and infuriated me.

Normally when I'm on a tennis court I'm completely oblivious to everything around me, but that afternoon I happened to catch a glimpse of some new arrivals out of the corner of my eye. What I saw almost made me drop my racquet right then and there. For a brief instant I swear I thought Chris Evert had strolled onto the court next to the one on which I was practicing.

It wasn't Chris, of course, but the young girl was practically a carbon copy, at least physically. She was accompanied by her mother, who did not look like Chris Evert.

The girl was about fourteen or fifteen years old, and she was wearing a Chris Evert tennis dress and carrying a Chris Evert tennis racquet. Her hair was the style and color of Chris', her fingernails were colored with a bright nail polish, and she was wearing bracelets and earrings, *à la* Chris Evert. I immediately got the impression the resemblance was more than mere coincidence, that it was meticulously planned.

By then I was very anxious to see the young girl play. I was having a difficult time concentrating on my workout because I was trying to keep an eye on what was happening next door.

The Evert look-alike and her mother finally unsheathed their racquets, opened a fresh can of balls, and took their respective places on either side of the net. I was really getting antsy now.

Mother and daughter began a baseline warm up and it was immediately obvious that both of them had played tennis before. Their warm-up shots were well-executed and crisp. Things were really getting interesting, especially when I noticed that the girl's poker-faced demeanor was eerily similar to Chris'.

For a full five minutes they hit nothing but forehands to each other, and the only communication that passed between them was a mumbled "sorry" on those rare occasions when a shot plowed into the net.

"Let's go," I thought to myself. "Let's see some backhands." At that point I would have been willing to bet anything that the girl had a two-fisted backhand. There was absolutely no doubt in my mind, but I wanted to see it. I wanted to see if the picture was indeed complete.

It was.

She had a two-fisted backhand alright, but it was terrible. She massacred the first backhand attempt badly.

"Concentrate," commanded the girl's mother.

The next attempt was only a slight improvement. All the grace that the girl had demonstrated on her forehands was missing. She suddenly looked clumsy and awkward. I couldn't believe it was the same person hitting those shots.

Her third backhand attempt sailed over her mother's head and thudded against the canvas backdrop. Up to then I had been fascinated, but what happened next infuriated me.

"How many times do I have to tell you to get close to the ball and to follow through?" said the mother angrily. "You're practically tripping over your own feet. Think about what you're trying to do, see if you can get it right for once."

I swear it was all I could do to keep from going over to the girl's mother and making her a necklace with my racquet.

The whole incident made me wonder just how much of the girl's Evert-like appearance was voluntary and how much of it was Mom's idea. It also made me think about all those other parents around the country who are devoting a lot of their energy toward turning their kids into something or somebody they're not.

Of course, tennis has always had it's fair share of tennis mothers and tennis fathers—the sport's equivalent of that well-known show biz phenomenon: stage mothers.

Tennis' versions of the stage mother treat their children like Barbie dolls. They dress them up, put tennis racquets into their chubby little hands, and force them to play tennis. They force them to take endless lessons. They force them to practice tennis for hours. They force them to compete in tournaments, and they try to force them to win those tournaments.

Why?

Often they do it as a means of fulfilling their own frustrated athletic desires; they are living vicariously through their children's performances and accomplishments. They're silently saying "I couldn't hack it [or "I was spending the peak years of my athletic life at a little get-together overseas known as World War II," or "If I hadn't gotten married and started a family when I did, I might have played at Wimbledon"] but, by God, I'm going to see that *you* get the chance I never had."

And the child? What if he or she doesn't particularly want that chance? What if he or she doesn't even like tennis? Well,

28

the tennis parent has an answer for that one, illogical though it may be: "Maybe my child doesn't truly appreciate what I'm doing for him (or her) right now, but he'll thank me someday."

Maybe a few unwilling victims of the hard-core tennis parent *will* thank them later. But most tennis parents will be lucky if their children are still speaking to them someday. And it will truly be a miracle if those youngsters ever pick up a tennis racquet when and if they finally extricate themselves from their parents' control.

Some tennis parents don't have to rely on overt force to make their children play tennis. Their "inducement" is more subtle but just as powerful as the strong-arm tactic. I'm speaking, of course, of that psychological force known as guilt.

In all fairness, I should point out that many tennis parents who end up using guilt to keep their children in the game are, in a sense, victims themselves. They don't usually preplan the situation; it just evolves. The following example of how a parent may make a child psychologically unable to quit playing tennis will show you what I mean.

A father casually asks his young son if he'd be interested in learning how to play tennis. The child immediately says yes. He knows his father plays, of course, and he leaps at the chance to please his dad—a perfectly normal response. Besides, the child thinks tennis looks like a lot of fun.

He enjoys his tennis lessons, but he likes the practice sessions with his father even more. Pretty soon he has developed into a pretty solid little player, and his father suggests that he sign up for a local tournament. The child thinks that's a great idea, especially when he wins his age division.

He is happy, naturally, but his happiness is barely a drop in the bucket compared to his father's joy. Dad is practically stopping people on the street to show them the tattered newspaper clipping that lists the age group winners, and he doesn't let more than an hour go by without reminding his son how proud he is. He starts talking about other tournaments, and the child is more than happy to oblige. For the next several months, father and son travel all over the state to various events. The child does pretty well most of the time, and he even wins one now and then.

But something's happening to the young player: He's beginning to dislike tennis. It happens slowly at first, but then the feeling accelerates rapidly. He no longer enjoys the pressures of competition, and he longs for the time when tennis was just him and his father on the court hitting balls and laughing a lot. He tries to put these feelings out of his mind and concentrate on winning tournaments and making his father prouder still, but it's no use. Tennis has lost its appeal.

A hundred times, maybe even a thousand times, he tries to tell his father that he wants to quit, but he can't quite make the words come out. If the father has noticed any sign of his son's disenchantment, he doesn't let on. Finally, in desperation, the child blurts out his feelings. His father's disappointment and shock is written all over his face, but then he smiles reassuringly.

"I can understand how you feel, Son," says the father. "We've been going pretty strong for a long time now. But all you need is a rest, and you'll be fine."

"I don't think so, Dad. I think it'd be better if I laid off tennis for a long time. Maybe even forever."

"Nonsense. You're just a little tired."

"Well . . ."

"So here's what we'll do. We'll forget about the tournament up north next weekend. That should give you plenty of time to recover. Then we'll throw ourselves back into the ol' tennis wars the week after."

"But . . ."

30

"You don't want to let your father down, do you?"

"No, of course not."

"Then it's all settled."

I'm sure you can figure out what's going to happen next. The child will continue playing because he doesn't want to "let his father down" or "disappoint" him. But he will probably be totally miserable, and in the end he may build up a tremendous resentment against his father.

Now there's absolutely nothing wrong with a parent encouraging a child to play tennis and to play it well, and there's absolutely nothing wrong with a parent who feels a certain amount of pride in a child's tennis accomplishments, whether on the tournament level or not. But . . . when the encouragement or pride becomes extreme enough to bind the child to tennis when he or she would rather not be playing, the parent is at fault.

A sensitive and understanding parent should, of course, try to avoid letting things get to the point where a child has to *ask* for permission *not* to play tennis, but if it does happen, the parent should have enough sense to go along with the child's wishes.

In our example, the child who eventually mustered up enough courage to verbalize his disillusionment with tennis wrestled with the problem of how to break the news for quite a while before actually doing so. The father and son also spent a lot of time together traveling to various tournaments so the father had ample opportunity to pick up on his son's failing interest. If he did notice that something was bothering the child, he should have tried to find out what it was, then and there. He should have approached his son and said: "You don't seem particularly enthused about playing in next week's tournament. Is something wrong?"

To which the son would reply: "Actually, there is some-

thing bothering me. Playing all these tournaments was fun at first, but I really miss the good times you and I use to have just fooling around on the court. Now when we practice it's all business because there's some dumb tournament I'm supposed to be getting ready to play. I don't know, tennis just isn't as much fun as it used to be."

The father could have responded with: "You're right. We did use to have fun, didn't we? And you know, I kind of miss it too. But we can fix that easy enough. We'll just stop running around as much and get back to having some fun."

Unfortunately, the father in our little scenario failed to

notice that something was bothering the child, and when he was finally told about it, he just brushed it off.

By doing so, he joined the legion of blatantly demanding tennis parents in violating the First Commandment of dealing with children and tennis: Children should only play tennis (or any other sport) because they *want* to, not because their parents want (or need) them to.

You, as a parent, should be encouraging and supportive, but never forceful or demanding. You should not expect or ask for a certain level of performance from your child other than that the young player perform to the best of his or her capabilities. And you should establish and maintain an open line of communication with your child. Listen to what they say and watch what they do. Children are adept at non-verbal communication, so their behavior can tell you quite a bit about feelings that they are either unwilling or unable to articulate.

Communication, after all, is the key to a successful parent/child relationship in all phases of a child's life, and that includes his or her athletic activities.

5

A Tennis Primer

A Brief Word on History

The very first time I hit a tennis ball I immediately discovered two things. The first, of course, was that I wanted to play tennis for the rest of my life. And the other? Well, my instant love affair with the game also taught me that I have a sense of history. I wanted to learn everything I could about tennis: where it came from; who had played it; and most of all, *how* they had played it. Toward that end, I began to devour everything I could find that had been written about tennis, which, at the time, wasn't a whole lot. Still, I was soon spending almost as much time reading about tennis as I was playing. And I spent *a lot* of time playing.

For most people who play, including many of today's pros, the mere fact that tennis exists is quite enough. They couldn't care less how it developed, and I think that's a mistake. Knowing a bit about the history of the game certainly isn't going to improve anyone's serve, but it can give them a deeper appreciation of what they're playing. For that reason alone, I would like to see parents encourage their tennis-playing offspring to familiarize themselves with the history of the sport and its pioneers.

Unfortunately, in the minds of many children (and adults too, for that matter) history is often synonymous with dryness, so it probably won't be the easiest thing in the world to convince them to check out tennis' past. It's not crucial to their enjoyment of the game, but it certainly won't hurt to give them a gentle nudge in that direction.

If successful, the results can be gratifying for both parent and child. The child will be pleasantly surprised to discover that history doesn't necessarily have to be the literary equivalent of the Sahara, and you will have the satisfaction of knowing your child is reading *something*. And what parent doesn't want that?

The Game

There is no such thing as a bad tennis player; some are merely better than others. ———A wise, old proverb of unknown origin.

Q: What exactly is tennis?

A: Tennis is a racquet sport involving a minimum of two players (singles) and a maximum of four players (doubles). "Triples" is not a recognized part of tennis, although a two-against-one alignment can be an effective practice drill for advanced players—it is also useful when a fourth fails to show up for a recreational doubles match.

A singles contest in any tournament or club-ladder contest features players of the same gender, but casual matches are often intersexual. Doubles fall into three categories: men's, women's, and mixed.

The game itself is played on a tennis court, a rectangular area of specified dimensions. All tennis courts are laterally bisected by a contraption known, appropriately enough, as a net. The net catches tennis balls. Unfortunately, however, the object of the game is not to hit the ball into the net, but over it. This should be uppermost in a player's mind at all times.

Of course, the net does more than just catch tennis balls. It divides the tennis court into two equal halves, each of which becomes the exclusive domain of the opposing players involved in a match. It is their turf, and they will alternately defend it and use it as a base from which to attack.

The players are not unarmed. They are equipped with a weapon that may be wielded with either the right or the left hand. The hand that guides the weapon in combat is usually determined by the player's involuntary proficiency with one hand or the other. Players favoring the left hand are known as "lefties" or "southpaws." Those favoring the right hand are known as the majority. There are some players of note, such as Jimmy Connors and Chris Evert, who occasionally grip their weapons with both hands, and there is at least one, Frew McMillan, who uses both hands almost all the time. But regardless of which hand does the gripping, the weapon, called a racquet, is absolutely essential to a tennis player. It is, after all, the implement with which the tennis ball is swatted. And successfully swatting the ball with a racquet is what tennis is all about.

Actually, swatting is a pretty unsophisticated word to use to describe the intricacies involved in propelling a tiny, rapidly moving sphere over a stationary barrier and into a designated area. It might be more appropriate to say that tennis balls are caressed, belted, sliced, spun, chipped, and . . . frequently mishit. Yes, "swatting" on a tennis court is an art; a constantly changing kaleidoscope of action and reaction.

Each swat, however, is an embellishment of one of half a dozen fundamental tennis strokes. By far the most common method of stroking a tennis ball is the groundstrokes: forehand and backhand. Groundstrokes are so named because contact is made with the ball after it has hit the ground. Groundstrokes are usually hit from deep in a player's turf. The volley is another fundamental tennis stroke. Volleys mean that the ball is struck *before* it bounces, and they are an integral part of a player's arsenal if he plans to spend any time in close proximity to the net.

The serve, of course, is the stroke that initially puts the ball in play, and then there are lobs, half-volleys, overheads, and, well, you get the picture.

Making contact with the ball is only the beginning of a successful shot, though. "Hitting it where they ain't" is a baseball cliché that also applies to tennis. Unlike the baseball player, however, it is both unwise and non-productive for a tennis player to hit it out of the park. Tennis requires a bit of restraint because a shot that fails to land within the well-defined boundaries of the court is worthless. Since the court is relatively small in area, hitting it where they ain't requires a lot of control and finesse. The player who manages to do so is rewarded with a point, the ultimate accolade for a single tennis shot.

Points are important because the object of the game is to accumulate them before your opponent does. Points win games, games win sets, and sets win matches.

Points can be earned by hitting the ball into the court beyond an opponent's reach or by presenting an opponent

NYAAH
NYAAH
NYAAH!

with a shot that is so well placed it is impossible to return. But points can be given up as easily as they can be earned. Maybe even more easily because there are more ways to lose points than there are to win them. The proper words for giving up points are "Uh oh." Translation: "How did I hit that easy forehand thirty feet past the baseline?"

Ah yes, the unforced error. The scourge of every human being who has ever stepped onto a tennis court. Unforced errors take several forms—double faults and hitting long, short, or wide are the most prominent—but the results are always the same: Frustration for the error and a point to the person on the other side of the net, the one trying to suppress a smirk. (It also happens that points are sometimes awarded erroneously by an impartial third party. And for some strange reason, it seems to happen only on crucial points. Of course, this phenomenon is restricted to tournament play that involves linesmen.)

One final thought about points: You can't win 'em all, but you should certainly try.

The Scoring

Consider, if you will, the following dialogue between two kids making their first visit to a tennis court. Try to ignore the fact that the dialogue is a complete fabrication.

FIRST KID: "Was it in?"

SECOND KID: "Yeah, but barely."

FIRST KID: "Barely's good enough. That gives me fifteen."

SECOND KID (*indignantly*): "That gives you fifteen what?"

FIRST KID: "I'm not sure. Fifteen points I guess."

SECOND KID: "Are you kidding? Fifteen points for one lucky shot? A touchdown's only worth *six* lousy points."

FIRST KID: "Yeah, I know. But tennis is different. The scoring is a little weird."

SECOND KID: "You're tellin' me. How did you learn about this 'fifteen' jazz, anyway?"

FIRST KID: "Don Budge explained it to me in a dream I had last night."

SECOND KID: "Don who?"

FIRST KID: "Don Budge. I don't know who he is, but he seemed to know what he was talking about."

SECOND KID: "Oh."

FIRST KID: "But wait, there's more."

SECOND KID: "Oh."

Though fictional, that little scene is not all that farfetched. Well, maybe the Don Budge part is, but the rest of it has undoubtedly occurred many times in many different places. There are not many things that make less sense than the disjointed tennis litany: love, fifteen, thirty, forty, game, deuce, advantage in, advantage out. But with all its mystique and colorful terminology, the sport's ancient scoring system adequately fulfills the function for which it was created. And it does so with a certain quaint charm.

Another bit of hypothetical dialogue, this time between parent and child:

CHILD: "Can I ask you something?"

PARENT: "Of course. What's on your mind?"

CHILD: "Not much. I just want to know where I came from, what caused the Crimean War, and why points in a tennis game are not simply called one, two, three, and four?"

To the latter question, the parent can respond with either a quizzical look and a mumbled "I don't know" (not a good

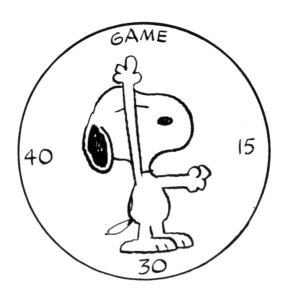

response) or a firm "Why don't you look it up" (a very good response).

The inquisitive child who does look it up will discover that one of the most common theories regarding tennis scoring dates back to the Middle Ages and is based on a measurement of time. A tennis game is symbolically related to an hour. Fifteen, the first point, is a quarter hour; 30 is the half hour; 40 (most likely it was originally 45) is three-quarters of an hour. Game point completed the sixty-minute analogy.

How "love" became part of the tennis lexicon is a matter of some conjecture, but many tennis historians believe it evolved out of the French word *l'oeuf,* meaning egg. In some circles, goose egg is a slang term for "no score" or "zero,"

which certainly lends credence to that theory. "Deuce" is probably derived from the French *à deux* or the Latin *duo.* "Advantage" more or less tells it like it is and requires no explanation.

Though the origin of the point designations is clouded,

their function is not. They are the very backbone of the sport's scoring system.

Basically, this is how the system works: Scoring in tennis consists of points, games, sets, and matches. A *game* consists of a minimum of four *points*, but there is no maximum. The player who wins the first four points (15, 30, 40, game) wins the game. If a game score goes to deuce (40–40), the eventual winner of that game will be the player who wins two consecutive points. The points that follow a deadlock at deuce are not numbered: They are called the "advantage" or "ad" points. It is subcategorized as either ad-in or ad-out, depending on whether the server or the receiver wins it. If the player who wins the advantage point also wins the next point, the game is over. If not, the score reverts back to deuce.

A *set* is awarded to the first player who wins six *games* with at least a two-game margin. This means that a game score of 5–5 in a set requires a player to win two more games before his opponent takes one. Obviously, open-ended sets, and the open-ended games that make up those sets, can result in tedious, marathon matches. A *match* is usually the best-of-three sets, but in some men's tournaments it may be the best-of-five sets.

A solution to the problem of excessively lengthy matches was adopted several years ago. Now, when a set is deadlocked at 6–6, a "tie breaker" is played (except at Wimbledon, which uses tie breakers when a set goes to 8–8 in all but the deciding set of a match).

Tie breakers come in several varieties. The most common are the nine-point "sudden death" and the twelve-point "lingering death." In the former, the first player to win five points is awarded the game and the set, while the latter requires a player to win at least seven points with at least a two-point cushion to emerge victorious.

Though it has been around for quite a while, tennis scoring has not been immune to criticism, and several progressively minded folks have attempted to simplify it. One of them, James Van Alan, the inventor of the nine-point tie breaker, has for years been trying to find acceptance for his No-Ad scoring system. In Van Alan's view, the sport would be greatly improved if the points were simply called "one, two, three, and four" and the deuce and ad points were discarded. No-Ad means exactly what it says: At 3–3, both players would be at game point.

World Team Tennis has used No-Ad scoring since the league's inception in 1974, and the system is spreading to college competitions and some exhibition tournaments.

There will be a quiz in the morning.

The Court

Though tennis courts appear to contain more lines than a Shakespearean soliloquy, the neophyte player should not be intimidated by the myriad of angles and intersections. After less than five minutes on a court, the terrain will be as familiar as the back of one's hand.

43

And, as far as the dimensions are concerned, once you've seen one tennis court, you've seen them all. Each and every one of them—from the famed Centre Court at Wimbledon to the long-neglected, severely cracked, chicken wire–bordered public court nestled among the tall pines near a tiny village in the Sierra Nevada mountains—is exactly 78 feet long and 36 feet wide. The latter figure includes the two 4½-foot doubles alleys that run the length of the court on either side. The doubles alleys are not used during singles play, thus reducing the singles court to a width of 27 feet.

The net, a loosely woven barrier that is 3½ feet high at the net posts but 6 inches lower at the middle of the court, is an integral part of every tennis court. A popular bit of tennis mythology holds that the net's sole purpose is to provide the winner of a match with something to jump over in jubilation, but, as I've already noted, its primary function is to prevent tennis balls from getting to the other side.

Adjacent to the net are four very important areas called service courts. There are two service courts on each side of the ball stopper. They measure 13½ feet by 21 feet and are crucial to getting the ball into play. The server, from a position behind the baseline, first serves into the deuce or the opponent's right court—that is, the service court to the server's left on the opposite side of the net. The next point commences when the server successfully places a serve in the ad or the opponent's left court. The server ignores the service courts on his or her own side of the court, and both players ignore the service courts once the ball is in play.

The portion of the court that lies between the sidelines and the service line and baseline is called the backcourt.

While the above dimensions may be unvarying, the surfaces into which they are inscribed are not. Tennis courts may be grass, cement, carpet, clay, asphalt, or cow dung.

44

A century ago, the sport was known as lawn tennis because, logically enough, it was played on grass almost exclusively. Over the years, however, grass courts have declined in number, mainly because of the constant maintenance they require. (They are still plentiful in a few countries though, including Australia and England. Most of the grass courts in this country may be found in the East.) Tennis courts of nature's carpet are classified as an extremely fast surface. This means the ball really moves.

Hardcourts, which are quite common in the United States, also play very fast. Hardcourts are usually made of cement, asphalt, or painted asphalt. Other than having to be washed down occasionally, they need little or no care and are therefore extremely popular with economy-minded municipal park administrators.

Most indoor tennis facilities utilize one of the several brands of carpet courts. (The Virginia Slims Circuit, for ex-

ample, uses a Sporteze surface.) All indoor carpet courts are fast, and they are portable. In a sense, they are a throwback to the generally recognized origins of lawn tennis. In 1874, an Englishman named Major Walter Clopton Wingfield, who is usually credited with "inventing" lawn tennis, took out a patent on a "new and improved *portable* court for playing the ancient game of tennis." Although he may be properly described as a visionary, Major Wingfield would undoubtedly be astounded by WTT's uniquely customized version of his "invention." The WTT surface, you see, has no lines at all. Instead, blocks of color separate the various areas of the playing surface: The doubles alleys are red, the deuce courts are blue, the ad courts are green, and the backcourts are chocolate brown.

Clay is the slowest surface. Calling all clay courts "clay," however, is like calling all tissues "Kleenex." In other words, they aren't always made of clay. A couple of years ago, for instance, the West Side Tennis Club at Forest Hills, New York, the site of the U.S. Open for many years, replaced all but a few of its grass courts with "clay." In actuality, the natural turf gave way to a clay-like substance called Har-Tru.

Clay courts are grainy and loose. They dry very quickly after a rain shower, create miniature dust bowls during gusty

winds, leave both ball marks and footprints, and require players to slide into shots like figure skaters. Since clay courts slow
the ball down, they are loved by players who grow up on
them, and often detested by players who learn the game on a
speedier surface.

Appellate courts, by the way, have absolutely no connection with tennis.

The Rules

It almost goes without saying that every tennis player, regardless of age, should be familiar with the rules of the game. That knowledge may be acquired by reading the "Official Code of the International Lawn Tennis Federation." The language of the Code is less than conversational though, and portions of it may require a bit of parental translation, especially for younger children.

It is probably safe to assume that only a tiny percentage of recreational players have actually sat down and read the official rules of tennis. Undoubtedly, most of them have picked up bits and pieces of information from several different sources: their instructor, experienced playing partners, and from observing matches on television.

Unfortunately, it is also probably safe to assume that many of these players are completely ignorant of several specific rules that could work to their advantage or avoid confusion when odd or infrequent situations occur during play. For example, is it ever possible to earn a point with a return that lands in your opponent's court *without* having cleared the net?

A trick question? Perhaps. But the answer is a firm, unequivocal "yes." If the ball is returned from outside the court, it is a good return even if it passes *below* the level of the net as long as it lands safely in the opposite court.

Another question: Is it ever permissible to reach across the net into an opponent's territory to hit the ball?

Again the answer is "yes." But only after the ball has first landed on your side of the court and then rebounds back over the net. Don't laugh, it happens. Not every day, of course, but it does happen. And the player who is suddenly put in the unique position of having to lean over the net to make contact with the ball must be careful not to touch the net. Doing so results in the automatic loss of the point.

It is always illegal to *reach* across the net to hit a volley, but if a player's racquet passes over the net *after* striking the ball on the proper side of the court, the return is good.

Suppose you are positioned near the baseline and your opponent hits an apparent fence-rattler that nicks your sleeve,

who gets the point? Your opponent does. It's right there in the Official Code, Rule 18, Section G.

A similar rule is the one that states if a server in a doubles

49

match hits the opposing team's net man with a serve, the point goes to the serving team. Strange but true.

Also, if the ball in play strikes a ball lying on the court, the ball in play remains in play.

These are just a few of the lesser-known tennis rules, but they, their application, and the application of all the rules, is neatly summed up by Rule 28 of the ILTF's Official Code. Rule 28 simply states that the rules apply to both sexes.

One more thing: Liners are good.

The Etiquette

Tennis etiquette may be described as the sport's version of table manners, and parents should make sure their children are familiar with common court courtesies.

The first thing a child should learn is that disrupting the

game on a neighboring court is a definite no-no. Occasionally, a ball will go astray and end up rolling across the court next door, but that is unavoidable and should not greatly upset the neighbors. But . . . if it happens every few seconds or if a child interrupts the play on an adjacent court to retrieve an errant ball, some harsh words may result. And rightfully so.

Children should also be taught not to walk behind or near players during a point.

Distractions can also be heard as well as seen. While communication by hand signals is not really necessary, court noise should be kept at a reasonable level.

Court etiquette during play consists mainly of treating an opponent in the same way you would like your opponent to treat you. (Sound familiar?)

Since linespersons are rarely used during a casual match, the players involved must assume the additional burdens of calling the shots and keeping score. Usually, the player closest to the ball makes the call. If it's out, the call should be made loudly, clearly, and quickly. If there is a question as to whether a ball is good or not, say so immediately and replay the point. It is obviously bad form to play out a point and then say, "You know, I think that lob was slightly long."

The server is responsible for remembering the score. At this point, I feel obligated to say that cheating on calls is thoroughly reprehensible. Though self-officiating during a match offers plenty of opportunity to "miss" calls on purpose, the player who does so has obviously missed the point of the game. Cheating may help to win a match now and then, but it won't quite offset the loss of self-respect that's bound to surface sooner or later.

Of course, 99.9 percent of all tennis players don't resort to cheating, so those that do stand out like sore thumbs. The clever person may get away with it for a while, but as ol' Abe

Lincoln said, "You may fool all the people some of the time; you can even fool some of the people all the time, but you can't fool all of the people all the time." He wasn't talking about tennis but it still applies.

6

The Equipment

Every tennis player, from the rank beginner to the top pro, has at least one thing in common: a dependence on those items collectively known as tennis equipment, the tools of the trade, if you will.

Besides the tennis court itself, the basic provisions a player needs include a racquet, tennis shoes, tennis balls, and clothing. Each will be discussed in this section, as will a fifth category: the optional—but plentiful—accessories tennis has spawned in direct proportion to its growing popularity.

Since all of the above vary widely in price and quality, a bit of careful comparison shopping is recommended before buying. Fortunately, that shouldn't present any problem because tennis equipment may be purchased practically anywhere.

Tennis shops, not surprisingly, offer a wide selection of equipment, but so do department stores, discount emporiums, some flea markets, and trading stamp outlets. There is even a mind-boggling array of tennis-related novelty items that are available by mail order.

Just remember that with a little time, effort, and common

sense, a child may be properly and sufficiently outfitted with decent equipment *without* putting a deep dent in the family budget. Hallelujah!

The Racquet

A tennis player without a racquet is like a car that's missing an engine; no matter how good they look, neither one's going to go very far. In other words, the racquet is the single most important part of a player's personal paraphernalia. And the proper racquet can make a big difference in a player's ability to control the ball.

Precisely because this piece of equipment is so vital to the game, many people are surprised to discover that there is no such thing as a "standard" or "regulation" tennis racquet. Indeed, the official rules of the sport do not require racquets to conform to specifications of either size, weight, or material composition. This lack of official restraints will, of course, be immediately apparent to anyone in the market for a racquet.

How then does a parent choose the right racquet for a child? Trial and error? Reliance on pure luck? A computer printout comparing the available products? Actually, it's quite possible to make a knowledgable and correct selection without consulting a soothsayer. All it takes is an understanding of a few racquet facts.

Welcome to Racquet Anatomy 1A.

In the recent past, tennis racquets were made only of wood. Though wood is still one of the most popular types, racquets are now available in steel, fiberglass, graphite, plastic, or practically any combination of the above. About the only thing racquets are *not* made of is kryptonite.

Most racquets, wood or otherwise, weigh between 12 and 15 ounces and are 27 inches long. You won't find the actual

weight marked on an individual racquet, however. Instead, most of them carry the designations *L* (for light), *M* (for medium), or *H* (for heavy) on the handle.

Most racquets also carry the grip size on the handle. Grip sizes will vary between 4¼ inches and 5 inches in circumference.

In most cases, a 4⅜–4½ L will be the best racquet for a child, unless he or she happens to be a junior version of Bigfoot.

A good rule of thumb for determining the proper grip is to shake hands with the racquet. (Saying something like "Nice to meet you" is not really necessary though.) This gesture is more than a mere courtesy. While shaking hands with the racquet, check the position of the thumb. If it meets the first knuckle of the second finger, the grip is acceptable. If the thumb overlaps the knuckle, the grip is too small; if it falls short, the grip is too large.

Some companies put out "junior" racquet models, and one of these cut-down models might be appropriate for younger children. Junior racquets are not exactly miniature versions of regular racquets, however. In fact, most are only slightly shorter (usually 26 inches) and only an ounce or two lighter than the 27-inch model. Most of the smaller racquets have a 4¼-inch grip. Besides the lightness and smaller grip, a junior racquet will put less strain on a child's elbow when contact is made with the ball than will a longer racquet. It will also give the very young, or small, child a greater sense of comfort, feel, and control.

Another thing to look for when shopping for a racquet is balance. Some players prefer racquets that are top-heavy, while others, including myself, like the quickness of motion a light-headed racquet provides. I would recommend an evenly balanced racquet for children. To check the balance of an unstrung racquet, lay the throat across your forefinger and move your hand slowly toward the bottom of the handle. The balance point should lie about halfway between the bottom of the racquet head and the heel of the handle.

There is a great debate among tennis players as to which type of racquet is superior: wood or metal. (The composites are still fairly expensive and haven't yet challenged the wood or metal varieties in popularity among casual players. As a result, they are conveniently absent from the Great Debate—for now, anyway.)

I have played with both wood and metal, and I have won major tournaments with both, but I prefer wood by far. It is my feeling that a player who learns the game with a metal racquet never really learns how to hit the ball correctly. Metal racquets have a definite "trampoline" effect because all of the strings spring into action, so to speak; whereas with a wood racquet, only the shorter cross strings do the work. Consequently, a metal racquet tends to make an inexperienced player slap at the ball instead of hitting through it. Learning to hit through the ball with control should be a primary goal of every tennis player. And since the ball sits on the strings of a wood racquet a fraction of a second longer than it does with metal, the wood offers much more control.

How the racquet is strung and what it is strung with don't really matter very much in the beginning. Nylon is cheap and doesn't require a lot of care, and it should be adequate for the beginner. Gut, the other widely used stringing material, provides greater "feel," but that particular distinction can usually only be appreciated after years of playing. Besides, gut can be rather costly.

Specific string tension is a major concern for many top

players but it shouldn't concern a parent who is shopping for a child's first racquet. There is some evidence that specific string tension provides more psychological benefits than physical ones, so a factory string job will be fine for the beginner.

Okay. So you've finally found the right racquet for your child. It is light enough to be lifted and swung; the grip is comfortable, and it has a full complement of strings that don't sag. Now what?

Well, you can teach the budding young player that although tennis racquets don't have to be fed, they do require a certain amount of care if they are to remain in good shape. Tennis racquets should not be kept in the family deep freeze or left out in the rain. It is also not wise to let them bake on a sunlit windowsill or on the rear deck of the family buggy.

When not in use, they should be kept in a cool, moisture-free place.

Since most wood racquets are laminated, a racquet press is not necessary. The racquet cover will provide adequate protection.

All racquets should be stored in an upright position—it is difficult to pile things on an upright racquet. The best method of handling a racquet when it's not in use is to hang it from a hook or nail. Most racquet covers have a small loop at the top for just that purpose.

Besides encouraging your child to take good care of his or her racquet, you, as a parent, should also break the news that a racquet is not a magic wand. Unless it breaks in half or the strings disintegrate during play, the racquet cannot, and should not, be held responsible for botched shots. Children who fall into the habit of blaming the innocent, inanimate implement for putting the ball into orbit or for missing it altogether are only fooling themselves, and their progress will suffer. To paraphrase a popular bumper sticker from a few years back: "Tennis racquets don't miss shots, tennis players miss shots."

Finally, it isn't really necessary to spend a lot of money for a child's first racquet. Around ten or fifteen dollars should be sufficient. There's no guarantee that the child is going to be playing tennis for any length of time, and if the little bugger decides that tennis isn't such a hot game after all, you'll be stuck with an expensive memento of a passing fancy. It may even be possible to avert a needless expenditure altogether. Some tennis facilities lend racquets to beginning tennis students. If a child who starts out using a borrowed racquet gets bitten by the tennis bug, the instructor should be able to advise the parent as to the proper racquet to purchase for the budding player.

Balls

Though the rules of the game don't have much to say about tennis racquets, they are quite verbose when it comes to discussing the tennis ball. Rule 3 of the "Official Code of the International Lawn Tennis Federation" is quite explicit in its requirements of the fuzzy, little spheres:

> The ball shall have a uniform outer surface. If there are any seams they shall be stitchless. The ball shall be more than two and a half inches and less than two and five-eighths inches in diameter, and more than two ounces and less than two and one-sixteenth ounces in weight. The ball shall have a bound of more than 53 inches and less than 58 inches when dropped 100 inches upon a concrete base, and a deformation of more than .265 of an inch and less than .290 of an inch when subjected to a pressure of 18 lb. applied to each end of any diameter.

Phew!

Of course, most people, myself included, aren't in the habit of looking at tennis balls as technological marvels of minutely computed deformation factors and rebound qualities. Let the engineers worry about size and weight tolerance; I just want to experience that unbelievable feeling when the results of their calculations and labors meet the strings of my racquet.

William T. Tilden 2nd felt the same way. Tilden, arguably the best player the game of tennis ever produced, possessed a truly philosophical view of the tennis ball. In 1925, a full half century before Tim Gallwey gave us *The Inner Game of Tennis*, Bill Tilden wrote about the tennis ball in terms associated more with Zen masters than tennis players.

In his classic book, *Match Play and the Spin of the Ball*, Tilden offers this gem: "Let me suggest the ball for a moment as an individual. It is a third party in the match. Will this third party be on your side or against you?" He goes on to discuss the "edges" of the ball and how it will do exactly what the racquet tells it to do.

Hitting a specific "edge" of the ball to impart spin is naturally beyond the capabilities of the beginning player who is trying to make head-on contact, but the idea of thinking of the ball as a third party in the match is something every player should strive for. Doing so will help to focus attention on the ball. And, of course, Tilden's observation that the ball's trajectory, pace, and spin is determined by its brief meeting with the racquet strings should be kept in mind at all times.

While Bill Tilden was playing and writing about tennis with equal eloquence, one of his contemporaries, Henry Ford, was making quite a splash with his mass-produced automobile. The story is told that a factory foreman approached Mr. Ford one day to ask about painting the vehicles that were rolling off the assembly line. "I don't care what color you paint them," said Mr. Ford, "as long as it's black."

(Hang on. The connection with tennis balls will become obvious in a moment.)

For a long time, the automobiles that bore Henry Ford's name were available only in black. But somewhere along the line, they began to appear in different colors. It even got to the point where black Fords were few and far between.

So it was with tennis balls. (Aha!)

Until 1968, they came in only one color: white. That year (coincidentally, the same year "open" tennis became a reality), *yellow* tennis balls were introduced. And before long, the colorful balls became more popular than the standard white ones. Suddenly, tennis balls began to appear in orange and green and red, and the white ball became increasingly rare. Some tournaments, including Wimbledon, still use white balls, but you can spend months at the local courts without seeing one.

"Hey, look at that! Those people are playing with white tennis balls."

"White? Isn't that illegal or something?"

"Naw. Tennis balls always used to be white."

"You're kidding?"

No matter what color you decide on, however, your best bet is to buy heavy-duty balls. The nap, or fuzz, on these balls is designed for a long ball life so you won't have to shell out three bucks everytime someone in the family lines up a match. Unpressurized balls are also good because they are heavier and won't go dead as quickly as the pressurized variety.

Worn-out balls that have lost some of their liveliness shouldn't be thrown out though. They are ideal for practice sessions because it requires a certain amount of effort and follow-through to keep a "dead" ball in play. Just make sure that the balls aren't in a complete state of rigor mortis or they will put too much of a strain on a young elbow. Having a basket of worn but still usable balls will also allow you and your child to get the most out of a practice session; you won't have to waste a lot of time retrieving the balls after just a couple of shots.

Shoes

What can I say? You know and I know that children have this magical power that enables them to go through a pair of tennis shoes in less than thirty seconds . . . while they're sitting completely still.

I can still see my mother's face when I'd come in from another session at the court. My feet would be poking out of the brand new pair of shoes I'd laced up for the first time

only that morning, and she'd just stand there staring at my toes in disbelief. No, tennis is not particularly kind to footwear, especially when there's an active youngster laced into them.

Nevertheless, it's extremely important that a child be outfitted with a pair of good supportive tennis shoes, ones that won't break down his or her feet.

The shoes, which may be either canvas or leather, should be fitted to allow the foot some breathing room, but they should be tight enough to prevent the foot from sliding around too much. Too much freedom in the shoe, coupled with the fast starts and stops tennis demands, will quickly produce painful, Mt. Everest–sized blisters. Not good.

Tennis footwear for children is definitely one item where buying the best is advisable.

Clothing

I got my introduction into the wonderful world of tennis fashion not long after I began playing. It happened at my very first tournament, the Southern California Junior Championships at the posh Los Angeles Tennis Club. I had never been to an actual tennis club before, and I felt somewhat intimidated by the surroundings. I managed to win my first match fairly easily, but I lost in the second round later that same day. By then I was less awed by the club atmosphere, but I still felt a vague sense of uneasiness, like I didn't belong there.

And sure enough, I didn't. Well, at least my tennis outfit didn't according to the tournament director. Because I wasn't wearing a tennis dress, I was not allowed to pose with the other players for a group photograph.

You'd have thought I'd shown up in bib overalls and barefoot the way the tournament director acted. As far as I was concerned, I was dressed for tennis. But the crisp white blouse and beautiful tennis shorts my mother had made me didn't quite cut the mustard at the L.A. Tennis Club.

The pettiness of the whole bizarre situation absolutely astounded me, and I think that's when I first began to feel that the sport could use some loosening up.

And it has loosened up considerably.

Happily, tennis' unwritten but strictly enforced dress code has been relaxed over the years. Some of the more established tennis clubs still insist on "white only" playing duds, but colorful clothing has become the rule rather than the exception. It has even become common to see people wearing tennis apparel in supermarkets, beauty parlors, and PTA meetings.

Tennis fashions are now available in a dazzling array of styles and fabrics. What you wear depends on your personal preference and how much money you're willing to spend. Of course, the particular climate in your area should also help you determine what to buy.

Just keep in mind that an outfit that looks like a million dollars but inhibits movement isn't worth a dime on the court. Clothing that allows freedom to run, jump, and stretch is absolutely essential.

And unless there are regulations at your local courts concerning playing attire, a T-shirt and a pair of cutoff jeans will be just fine for a child.

Miscellaneous Accouterments

Just listing what's on the market in this category of equipment would practically fill an entire book. Some of the accessories are good; some are not so good; and some are downright useless.

Again, what you spend on accessories is up to you, but if you plan to pick up more than a few, you'll surely need something in which to carry them. In that case, a tennis utility bag should probably be your first purchase. Utility bags can be bought for as little as ten or fifteen dollars or as much as a round trip plane ticket to Hawaii. It all depends on whose name is attached to it.

If you're determined to fill your utility bag with some of the more useful tennis accessories, you'll want to start with a pair of terrycloth wristbands and maybe a matching headband (color schemes optional). These items are intended to keep your hands dry and the perspiration or your hair out of your eyes.

If the amount of perspiration you generate overloads your wristbands and headband, just reach for the small towel that's in your utility bag somewhere. The towel is also useful for wiping off the racquet handle between games.

If you live in a particularly sunny clime, you might also consider carrying a tennis visor or hat.

I could go on, of course, but I won't. Just try not to get carried away. After all, do you or your child really need a combination garment bag–racquet carrier or a gadget that measures string tension?

7

Toward a

More Healthy Body

Nutrition

Food. Great, glorious, energy-giving, often fattening food. The staff of life. Our daily bread. High octane fuel for the human body.

We all need it, and most of us, myself included, love it. In fact if we are, as they say, what we eat, I've spent a good part of my life as a hamburger/taco combo with a side of ice cream.

The world would be a far better place if over-the-counter burgers and other goodies —collectively known as junk food— were suddenly discovered to be the perfect nutritional program. But it's just not going to happen.

What we eat is, of course, directly related to how we feel and how we function at work, at school, and at play. A poor diet affects our minds as well as our bodies, so we must insure that we, and our families, are on the receiving end of a proper and healthy diet. Needless to say, it's not always easy.

Athletes, because of their intense body-consciousness, should be models of nutritional efficiency, and many are. But many others are not. Athletes are human beings first, and they are not immune from becoming dietary derelicts.

I'm speaking, now, from personal experience. Only fairly recently did I come to fully understand the importance of eating properly. I only wish it had happened twenty years earlier. Oh, I suppose, like most people, I knew that eating the proper foods was something to strive for, but I didn't make much of an effort to do so. I guess I just wasn't a real believer. I usually thought of food only in terms of taste, convenience, and how much excess baggage it would plaster on the ol' hips and thighs. My program of nutrition consisted of eating pretty much what I wanted, with occasional periods of forcing myself to forsake a few especially tasty frills such as ice cream and

beer. At such times, I felt I was taking candy from a baby, and I was the baby!

In an admittedly weak defense of my eating habits, I can only say that I've had plenty of company in my ignorance or disregard for proper nutrition. Consider the practice of football players who claim that devouring a big steak before the game helps them build up enough energy to devour the opposition. It certainly sounds good, but while the steak-fed behemoths are knocking heads on the gridiron, their bodies are knocking themselves out trying to keep that pre-game slab of meat down. The digestive process is just warming up long after the final gun has sounded. So much for quick energy from the training table.

I'm not going to suggest a specific diet for you or your child, but I will say that it should be well balanced, eaten at regular intervals, and light on the junk. Extremely light. The earlier children develop good eating habits and acquire a knowledge of what's healthy and what's not, the better off they'll be.

If there is a cardinal rule regarding food consumption, it is that refined sugar, refined starches, and the products containing those ingredients should be avoided as much as possible—specifically, white bread, white sugar, and many processed snacks. They are not only nutritionally worthless, but they are harmful to one's health.

Look at it this way: If you put sugar in your car's gas tank it will stop running. Well, the same principal applies to the human body.

It is somewhat alarming, therefore, to discover that we as a nation are in the firm grip of a phenomenon that has been called the "White Plague." In other words, we are overdosing on the nutritional vacuum created by an abundance of sweet-tasting products that are saturated with refined sugars and starches. A 1974 Department of Agriculture survey indicated that every man, woman, and child in the United States, excluding military personnel, consumed approximately 99.7 *pounds* of refined *sugar* a year.

Not surprising, many doctors attribute our high national incidence of heart disease and other ills to this extremely harmful dietary idiosyncracy. And, of course, the family dentist sees a steady stream of casualties.

But here's the ironic part. Sugar is a carbohydrate, and carbohydrates are unbeatable as energy-providers because they supply the body with instant calories. They stoke the fire, so to speak, and this leaves the protein free to keep the body in good repair instead of being burned up for energy.

What all this means is that increasing the carbohydrate intake before playing tennis is a good idea. Don't start laying in a supply of potato chips, cookies, or cream-filled chocolate fudgies, though. Refined carbohydrates won't do it.

Fortunately, there are plenty of *unrefined*, nutritionally beneficial carbohydrates that will. Dry fruits, pure unpasteurized honey, nuts, raisins, and natural cereals fall into the category of high-energy, healthy carbohydrates.

Earlier I said that the racquet is a tennis player's most important piece of equipment, but I take that back. Racquets, and every other piece of equipment, rank far behind a tennis player's *body* in importance.

After all, that's one item that cannot be replaced.

Conditioning

Anyone who's seen *The Sound of Music* might remember that conditioning wasn't mentioned as being among Julie Andrews' favorite things. Well, I'm with Julie. In fact, if I were to sit down and compose a list of my favorite things, root canals and running out of gas on the Hollywood Freeway at rush hour would rank well ahead of conditioning. I dislike training almost as much as I like food that isn't good for me.

Conditioning, training, exercising, or whatever name it assumes, is seldom a barrel of laughs, but it is *always* hard work. It's also the one *sure* way to get the complex machine known as the human body into good shape. Providing, of course, that it is done on a regular basis.

If the very word "exercise" strikes terror into your heart, you're a certified member of the majority. But unless you're also a certified member of that tiny minority who are able to spend a few hours a day on the tennis court, I'm afraid you're stuck with exercise until something better comes along.

The plain and simple truth is that some form of regular exercise or physical fitness should be part of everyone's life. Adults, however, usually have a greater need for a regimented conditioning program than children, who normally lead more active lives. But children should be encouraged in the area of physical conditioning regardless of the extent of their participation in sports. Besides getting the body into shape, proper exercise can go a long way toward preventing such injuries as torn muscles or ligaments.

Once the body is in shape, tennis can help keep it there, especially as the skill level improves. As the level of play rises, the ball is kept in play for longer periods of time and more running is required. Hitting the ball isn't the main physical benefit tennis provides; getting to the place where you are in a position to hit the ball is. Played properly, tennis is a series of short, 5- and 10-yard dashes that, taken together, demand a lot of endurance. But the key is running. The game must be played vigorously if it is to have a positive or sustaining effect on fitness.

Since endurance or stamina is tied directly into the heart, it follows that increasing the cardiovascular capacity will result in an increase in endurance. Enlarging the cardiovascular capacity is accomplished only when the heart is "overloaded" for brief periods of time. This increased capacity translates into stamina because the heart pumps the oxygen and oxygen is the combustible agent that causes the carbohydrates and fats to ignite. Burned up carbs and fats equal energy, and energy means that maybe, just maybe, you'll be able to run down that crosscourt drop shot during the third-set tie breaker.

A strong heart will not be harmed by intermittent "over-loading," either during a conditioning workout or an actual tennis match, but a weak one might be. It's a good idea, there-fore, to have a doctor confirm you're in general good health before embarking on any strenuous exercise program, espe-cially if you're over thirty-five and are coming off a lengthy period of relative inactivity.

And remember that different individuals have different needs. Find out what's best for you and the other members of your family and build gradually. Physical fitness is not an over-night miracle worker.

Before going any further, I would like to discuss a related topic that has long been a chief concern of many people. I am referring, of course, to body weight.

For years, we've been inundated with warnings that we are turning into a nation of El Chubbos, and there is ample evidence that perhaps the charge is not overblown. Body weight, however, is not nearly as important to physical fitness as is the percentage of *body fat*. A svelte, 110-pound housewife who's carrying around a load of 20 percent body fat may look terrific, but she's a long way from being in good shape.

My weight has been known to fluctuate from time to time, but I've learned that if I get the body fat content down to around 9 percent I feel better physically than when I weigh less but have twice as much body fat.

People who are experts in such matters generally agree

that an athlete should have no more than 10 percent body fat, but when I was first measured a few years ago, I was at 13½ percent. Since I was also actively playing tennis at the time, we can safely assume that the national average is probably much higher. Nutrition and exercise is the only answer to the dual problem of excess body weight and body fat. With the proper education in these areas, it's entirely possible that today's children won't wake up one day thirty years from now and face the chore of restructuring their life-styles in deference to their health.

Meanwhile, back to conditioning. A good way to start is to convince yourself and your family that exercising is fun. Organize a daily family exercise period, not because misery

loves company but because exercising is so much fun that it should be shared by all. (Ha!)

I've also found that music can be a great morale booster while working out. Choose something that's upbeat but make sure you stay away from chain-gang songs. They may hit too close to home. I would also advise against *forcing* children to take part in home exercise sessions. If they're reluctant to participate, just let them see how much fun a dozen push-ups can really be. (Academy Awards have been handed out for less demanding roles.) Chances are, they'll come around before long.

The following conditioning tips, which are designed for the tennis player, are provided by Joanne Taylor, women's physical fitness director at the Southwest 1 Racquet Club in Montreal, Canada.

I have been putting my aching body at Joanne's mercy since 1974, and she has done a truly amazing job of teaching me how to keep myself in Grade A, prime condition.

Since it is extremely difficult to be specific when discussing conditioning programs for children (because they differ in strength, attention span, motivation, and goals), I asked Joanne to deal, instead, with the principles of conditioning. The basic ingredients she offers here should, however, provide you with the makings of a highly beneficial tennis conditioning program for your child and yourself.

A conditoning program for the young tennis player should encompass the following areas:

Strength (head to toe)
Flexibility (head to toe)
Endurance (both long and short term)
Footwork
Eye/hand coordination
Grip and forearm strength

Methods

Strength—calisthenics and weight training

Flexibility—stretching exercises, yoga (see Warming Up section for specific exercises)

Endurance (long term)—long runs or bike rides

(short term)—interval sprints, tennis court drills

Footwork—any drills involving moving the feet quickly

Eye/hand coordination—volley drills on the court

Grip and forearm strength—squeezing towels, balls, or grip machines, as well as wrist curls with weights

At this point, two very important training principles must be emphasized: interval training and overload principle.

Interval training refers to a period of work, followed by a period of rest. This pattern should be repeated several times. Rest periods should never allow for complete recovery, however! Improvement is attained by increasing the number of work periods, decreasing the length of the rest periods, or both.

This is one of the most important training methods for tennis players because it relates to what happens on the court during play. A point is played, a short break is taken, another point is played, another break is taken, and so on. Tennis is a game of intense effort broken up by short rest periods.

Examples of interval training on the court:

Two on one drills in which two players run one player around the court for one minute. This is followed by a 30 second rest and then another minute of strenuous activity. Repeat until the single player has gotten a good workout.

Take twenty tennis balls to the court and stand on one side of the net at the service line. Hit the balls to different spots on the court while your child tries to place the returns to a designated area. Don't make any attempt to return the balls. After hitting the twenty balls, rest 30 seconds, then repeat. Do this approximately six times and you'll have a very tired child on your hands, but one who's on the way to being in excellent condition.

Run pre-designated patterns on the court, concentrating on moving the feet quickly. Run for 30 seconds, rest for 15, and repeat.

NOTE: Longer, slower runs are an important part of training, but they do not specifically prepare a child for the short, intense bursts required on the tennis court. A combination of long runs and a *lot* of interval training on the court is a good idea.

The *overload principle* of training means that when working on strength or endurance, improvement occurs when the workload is beyond that to which the individual is accustomed. It's that extra effort that really counts. In other words, when you feel like stopping, it's time to do one more!

Important Conditioning Considerations

Do as much training as possible *on the court*. This will improve skills while improving the physical condition.

Make it fun, especially with younger kids.

Circuit training should be utilized as often as possible. Basically, circuit training means that calisthenics, footwork drills, or stretching exercises are combined into defined routines. Put several exercises together and go through them several times.

Encourage your child to use his or her bicycle as a training device. Cycling builds endurance and strong legs, a must for tennis. It also strengthens the knees.

Go until it feels tough, then do a few more. This is a general rule of conditioning. But let your child discover his or her own limits. It is usually better to use time limits rather than specific numbers when exercising. Twenty sit-ups might be easy for one child, but impossible for another. With a time limit, however, a weaker child will not become discouraged as easily.

Recognize individual differences. Some kids will need a push, some will need a lot of praise. Try to make sure each and every child derives a sense of accomplishment from the training session.

The intensity of the training depends on the age, strength, and objectives of the child. Don't overdo it.

Avoid deep crouches, deep squats, and bouncing. These exercises are particularly tough on the knees and especially on very young knees or joints. Also, repetitive jumps on a hard surface are bad for the knees and shins.

Conditioning Exercises

RUNNING:

Long runs If possible, avoid running on pavement because doing so is hard on knees and shins. Also try to avoid running up and down hills. This, too, can be very bad for the knees and the Achilles tendon. Run *softly* and with *short strides*.

Short bursts This can be done anywhere, of course, but it is especially helpful to run patterns on a tennis court.

CYCLING:

Excellent for endurance and legs. Stationary bikes are ideal training devices if cycling in the street is difficult.

CALISTHENICS FOR GENERAL BODY STRENGTH:

Push-ups It's fine for younger kids to do push-ups, but to the knees only. The knees stay on the ground at all times.

Sit-ups Should be done with the knees *bent* and with support on the feet if possible.

Prone arch Lie on your stomach with your hands behind

76

your back. Lift chest and both legs simultaneously. *Do not force* the arch in your back. This is to strengthen the back, not stretch it.

Heel raises Standing, go up and down from a flat foot to your toes.

Side leg raises Lying on your side, keep lower knee bent and raise and lower the straight upper leg.

LEG EXERCISES:

Lunges Stand with feet together. Take a big step, bend the knee and *push off* the front leg back up to the standing position. When doing this one, don't go too low. Bend the knee so the thigh is not quite parallel to the ground and no further. Alternate legs.

Shifting Stand with feet wide apart. Shift your weight from side to side, putting all your weight on one foot, then push off and shift weight to the opposite foot. Sit back slightly while doing this one, but don't crouch too low.

Ball pick up Spread twenty balls around the floor (or court) and pick them up as quickly as possible bending from the knees.

Squat walk Squat down (again, not too low) and walk around for a few minutes.

WRIST AND FOREARM EXERCISES:

Towel grip Roll up a towel. Hold it with both hands and with elbows slightly bent, grip, release, grip, release. Do for one minute.

Wrist curls Sit down and put forearms on thighs to stabilize them. With the palms up, hold any weight (books, racquet bags, etc.) and curl wrists up. Repeat until tired. Then, with palms facing down, curl the wrists back. The forearms should remain motionless.

FOOTWORK EXERCISES:

Fast footwork Stand on a spot and move your feet as fast

as possible. While running in place, try not to kick your knees up too high. Do this for about 15 seconds at a time. Speed counts in this one.

Crossovers Similar to fast footwork exercise, but the feet should step across each other alternately.

Racquet jump Place a racquet on the floor and put your feet together. Now jump over the racquet from side to side as quickly as possible. Try to land lightly on your feet after each jump.

Skipping Again, speed counts. Skip quickly and lightly for a short period of time, rest, and repeat.

A Final Word about Conditioning

It is very important that you be concerned about your child's total body conditioning and not just his or her tennis skills. The stronger and more fit the child, the better he or she will be able to execute those skills.

Warming Up (and Down)

Being in excellent physical condition is something we should all aim for whether we play tennis or not. But having reached it doesn't mean that a tennis player is automatically ready to step onto the court and go all out on a moment's notice. Even players who are in top physical shape require a period of warming up before playing. This is something every child should be made aware of, but merely telling them that warming up is important probably won't do a whole lot of good unless they are also told *why* it's important.

Basically, there are two phases to warming up. The first phase consists of getting the body ready to absorb a round of physical exertion. The muscles must be prepared for the job of running, leaping, and stretching if they are to be expected to function in a manner that approaches maximum efficiency. Cold muscles may be up to 20 percent less efficient than warm ones, and if they are caught totally by surprise, there's a good chance they'll rebel against the sudden strain. When that happens, a cold muscle might decide to protest the unfair treatment by tearing or getting pulled. When a muscle is torn or injured in some way, the owner of that muscle will find out about it in a hurry. Warming up won't completely eliminate the possibility of such injuries, but it will certainly lower the odds. A player who skips a warm up greatly increases the risk of being put out of action for a while.

Both adults and children should acquire the habit of warning their bodies that a bit of exertion is just around the corner. A series of stretching or limbering up exercises should, therefore, precede a full steam effort on the court.

The second phase of warming up for tennis occurs on the court itself. While the players involved are running through the basic strokes (groundstrokes, volleys, overheads, and serves) the muscles are being warmed up further, but the players' timing, racquet control, and eye for the ball are also being sharpened.

A player may work out every day without fail, but a week or two away from the court will necessitate a bit of fine-tuning on both the timing and the swing. An organized warm up period can go a long way toward bringing a game back into proper focus.

Normally, a couple of minutes of off-court exercise coupled with 10 minutes of on-court ball contact and fast footwork exercises will adequately prepare the player and his body for a strenuous session of tennis. Of course, the warm up time needed increases or decreases depending on the weather conditions. It takes longer to warm up on a cold day than it does on a warm one.

Warming up *before* playing shouldn't be a player's only concern, however. A "warm down" period *after* playing is also a good idea. The great majority of recreational players never take the time to spend a few minutes warming down after practice or a match, but they'd be doing themselves a favor if they would.

Again, just a few post-playing exercises will help to relax the muscles and keep them flexible.

Try it and I promise you that if your muscle fibers could talk, they'd say, "Thank you."

The following specific warm-up exercises are suggested by Joanne Taylor. The number of repetitions is meant as a guideline only. The important thing is to do the exercises until you feel their effect. A proper warm up should work up a bit of a sweat, but it definitely should *not* tire you out.

Warm-Up Exercises

Arm circles Move arms in circles, both directions (15 each way).

Shoulder rotations Rotate shoulders, both directions (6 each way).

Knee lifts Standing, pull one knee to the chest, then the other (8 each leg).

Heel raises Standing, raise up and down on toes (20).

Trunk twisting Standing, hands behind head, twist trunk from side to side (20).

Vertical arm lifts Standing, arms at side, lift arms straight up in front and over head (20).

Lateral arm lifts Standing, arms at side, lift arms out to side and up over head (20).

Sidebends Standing, hands behind head, smoothly bend from side to side (20).

Head turns Turn head from side to side (20).

Bent knee sit-ups While lying on back with hands behind head, knees bent, and feet supported, sit up (10).

Elbow-knee touch and twist Standing, alternately touch right elbow to left knee, left elbow to right knee, while lifting knees high and twisting torso (50).

Stretching Exercises

Stretching exercises should be included in the daily training regimen as well as the pre-playing warm-up routine. All stretching should be done slowly, smoothly, and held for at least three slow counts. Stretch to the point of feeling it, but be careful not to overstrain. Do at least five repetitions of each stretch.

Tennis is a one-side-of-the-body sport, and when muscles are overused they become tight. To keep the young (or older) player loose, and to prevent possible injuries, stretching exercises are a must. Just be careful to avoid bobbing or bouncing.

Inside thigh and waist stretch Stand sideways to a chair or bench, put one foot up on the seat keeping both legs straight, clasp hands behind the head, and bend sideways toward the chair.

Thigh and shoulder stretch Stand with feet apart and hands clasped behind back. Bend forward, head to knees, to stretch the back of the thighs. At the same time, pull hands up to stretch the shoulders.

All over stretch Get down on all fours. First, lift rear end up and tuck head in while pushing heels *down*. This will stretch the calves and Achilles tendon. Then, keeping arms straight, arch the back and pull your head back. These two movements should be done slowly and smoothly.

Calf stretch Stand facing a wall or fence; lean against it while keeping the body straight. Push heels down and let your rear end sag in toward the wall or fence.

Hurdle sit stretch Sit down with one leg straight and the other bent at the knee as if jumping a hurdle. Bend forward, trying to touch forehead to the knee of the straight leg. Alternate legs.

Back arch Lie on stomach, hands under shoulders, palms down. Slowly push up with arms, arching the back. Put head back and stay in the arched position. Hold for a three count, then let your head drop forward and hold this position for a three count. Finally, lower to prone position.

Seated torso twist Sit on anything that's handy and clasp hands behind head. Twist torso from side to side as far as possible and hold. Turn head in direction of each twist.

Two-way shoulder stretch One, with hands clasped, raise both arms up over head. Pull hands back, stretching the shoulders, but don't arch back while doing this. Two, hold arms out straight from shoulders and move hands back, keeping them at shoulder height.

8

Getting Your Child

Started

Beginnings

There is no such thing as the "perfect" age when a child should begin playing tennis. I had my first experience with the game just before I turned eleven and that was, if anything, too late for me; for someone else, it might have been too early.

As a result of the increased awareness of tennis at every age level, more and more children are taking up the game much earlier than I did, but "the sooner the better" isn't necessarily always best.

Tennis, like music and mathematics, has seen its share of child prodigies, but, generally speaking, children under eight or nine years of age will probably not derive a great deal of pleasure from the sport. The fundamentals and basic strategies will most likely exceed their grasp in the figurative sense of the word, and the racquet will probably be too heavy and unwieldy for their grasp in the literal sense.

So rather than putting a tennis racquet in the baby's crib or dragging the toddler out to the court when he or she is barely able to put together a half dozen unaided steps, a

parent will be better off concentrating on less demanding physical activities at first. And so, might I add, will the child.

Playing catch, for instance, will have a far greater impact on a child's future proficiency on a tennis court than will, say, having him practice swinging a tennis racquet "just to get the feel of it." And not only will tossing a ball back and forth be more fun for the child, it will help to develop the hand/eye coordination that is a valuable asset for a tennis player. In addition, the child who learns to throw a ball properly will usually have less trouble with the tennis serve than the child who never developed a natural throwing action. Serving a tennis ball and throwing a baseball or football require similar body movements. The obvious difference is that a tennis ball is thrown by an extension—the racquet—rather than by the hand.

Although very young children may find the actual game of tennis beyond their physical abilities and, therefore, somewhat dull and unappealing, five- or six-year-olds who demonstrate an interest in tennis and are constantly asking for a chance to hit the ball should not be discouraged from trying to do so. Fortunately, the insistent child's desire can be satisfied without having to tie up a tennis court; the backyard will serve as an adequate substitute. Just grab a racquet, a bucket of used balls, and turn the backyard belter loose. Any discussion of technique, aside from making sure the child knows which end of the racquet to hang on to and that keeping an eye on the ball is a good idea, should be studiously avoided at this point.

The main idea, of course, is to stress contact and nothing more. Any contact may be rightfully considered a major accomplishment; anything resembling contact with *control* may be considered a miracle of immense proportions.

Tossing tennis balls to an eager, but usually unskilled, five-year-old may not be one of the most exciting things in the world, so you'll need an ample supply of patience and tennis balls. But when the magic moment finally arrives and the child makes contact with the ball—and it will arrive—the effort suddenly becomes worthwhile.

Over the years, I've participated in countless tennis clinics and the high point for me always comes when I see youngsters who're not much bigger than a racquet hit a ball for the first time. When it happens, a grin as wide as the baseline plasters itself on their faces and they start hootin' and hollerin' like you wouldn't believe. And their joy is total and contagious.

Lessons

"Close the gate!"

With those three words ringing in my ears, I began my formal tennis education one sunny Tuesday afternoon in September 1954. I know it was a Tuesday because the instructor, a man named Clyde Walker, gave lessons at a different Long Beach municipal park each day, and Tuesday was his day at Houghton Park.

I can still remember each detail of my first tennis lesson—

from Clyde's opening remarks about closing the gate (the first rule of tennis) to climbing into our family car when it was over and telling my thoroughly astonished mother that I was going to be the Number One tennis player in the world someday. (No kidding, I really said that.)

Three other girls were at Houghton Park that day for lessons, and although they were all four or five years older than me, they weren't any bigger than my 125 pounds. Clyde was definitely surprised and more than a little pleased when I told him I was only ten years old. I think my obvious enthusiasm pleased him as well.

Before coming to the Long Beach Rec Department, Clyde had taught tennis for many years at various country clubs, but he didn't feel his young club students were serious about tennis. Apparently a lot of them showed up for lessons only because their parents demanded it, and Clyde finally got fed up and quit.

Well, that certainly wasn't a problem on the municipal park courts. We showed up because we *wanted* to play tennis. At least I did.

That first day Clyde taught me the Continental grip, which is the same for both forehand and backhand, and showed me how to swing through the ball. After I had executed, and I do mean executed, a few swings at a phantom ball, he handed me a beat up practice ball and told me to drop it with my left hand and hit it after it had bounced. I spent the rest of the lesson time dropping balls and hitting them, or at least most of them, over the net while Clyde stood nearby critiquing my swing. I was in seventh heaven the whole time, and I didn't come in for a landing until long after I got home. I knew it was just the beginning, that there would be another lesson, and another, and another, and . . . well, that certainly pumped me up.

I immediately became a Houghton Park regular, but an

hour a week of Clyde's instruction wasn't nearly enough for me. I wanted, *needed*, more. Before long, Jerry Cromwell, a buddy and a fellow tennis fanatic, and I began showing up at Clyde's lessons all over Long Beach. We figured that if a doctor only makes house calls on Tuesday, but you need one on Monday, Wednesday, Thursday, and Friday, then your only option is to visit the doctor's office. And that's exactly what we did.

I was incredibly lucky to find a man like Clyde Walker. In many ways he was one-of-a-kind, but there are a lot of equally dedicated, qualified, intelligent, and sensitive tennis instructors around today.

Before discussing how to make sure your child is handed over to a competent tennis teacher, however, I want to say a few words about lessons in general.

Though I am a product of a group lesson program, I think I can objectively say that group lessons are preferable to individual or private sessions for beginners of all ages, but especially for children.

For one thing, group lessons are not nearly as expensive as private lessons. Luckily, I never had to pay for a tennis lesson in my life, and free group lessons, though dying, still exist in some municipal park systems. Free private instruction, however, is about as rare as an uncooked steak.

And even when a fee is charged for a group program, it is usually anywhere from one-fourth to one-tenth the cost of a private session. If your child spends a half-hour with a club pro, it will probably set you back ten to fifteen dollars, which is about what you should have paid for a young student's first racquet. A similar session with a non-affiliated "pro," usually someone who used to play on the college team and is teaching part-time to pick up extra money, will only cost between five and ten dollars. The tab will also be close to that amount if your local rec department offers individual instruction.

Group lessons at the club will run somewhere around three to five dollars *per hour* per student, and a *full schedule* of from six to twenty sessions is available for ten to fifty dollars through many recreation departments. (Groups are divided into skill—beginner, intermediate, advanced—and age levels.)

A lot of people are under the misconception that individual instruction automatically insures that a player will enjoy more progress. That's not necessarily true. A player who's attained a fairly high skill level may require individual attention at some point if progress is to continue, but the beginning player will be much better off in a group learning situation.

Besides placing children squarely in the middle of a social situation where they can interact with others, a group lesson gives them an opportunity to observe other children struggling to hit a tennis ball. As a result, they will immediately be comforted by the knowledge that they are not the only ones in the world who are a long way from being ready to challenge Jimmy Connors or Chris Evert. The child enrolled in private lessons, however, operates in a vacuum of sorts. The instructor will be full of helpful suggestions, of course, but all the child knows is that tennis is not as easy as it looks. And despite the instructor's constant assurances that he or she is doing very well, the child just might become convinced that anybody could do better.

Although the mutually shared struggles, frustrations, and successes inherent in a group situation can be extremely beneficial, group lessons are also superior to private lessons as a teaching vehicle. The absence of constant individual attention is more than compensated for by the chance to learn from the mistakes of others.

When I was making the rounds of the Long Beach park

90

system, watching the other students quickly became an invaluable part of my learning process. For example, Clyde might have mentioned that on my forehand I was waving my racquet around like Old Glory. And while I was working on getting rid of that problem, I might hear him tell someone else in the group the same thing. I would then make it a point to carefully watch that person. More often than not, actually seeing my flaw in someone else would help me get straightened out.

Similarly, an attentive child can learn a great deal merely by listening to what the instructor says to others during a group lesson. In a sense, therefore, a group learning environment may be described as a series of individual lessons.

Since the younger child's attention span is fairly short, I would advise parents to enroll them in a lesson program that features teaching sessions no longer than a half-hour per day. A half-hour lesson provides a sufficient amount of time for a child to absorb the principles of a new concept and to practice it under the watchful eye of the instructor. An hour lesson might very easily end up boring the child, especially in the beginning.

Though it is my firm belief that parents should refrain from teaching tennis to their children, I also feel that parents should not hang around to watch their children's lessons. Parents who take an active interest in their child's tennis development are to be applauded, but hovering around the court while a lesson is in progress may severely inhibit or distract a young player. The child will be less self-conscious if Mom or Dad disappears when the lesson begins, and the instructor will be more effective if he or she is dealing with a student whose attention is not divided.

I'm not trying to insinuate that a parent's involvement with his or her child's tennis career be restricted only to shelling out the dough for equipment and lessons. Far from it. The parent can and should assume the role of a practice partner.

Nobody really learns tennis from a series of half-hour lessons; they learn by spending a lot of time *practicing* what they've been shown. Obviously, the practice sessions should complement the lessons by concentrating only on those areas of the game the child is familiar with at any given time.

Avoid scenes like:

"Okay. I'll hit up a few lobs so you can work on the ol' overhead."

"The *what?*"

"The overhead. You know, the sure-point smasheroo."

"Do I have to, Dad? I mean, today was only my first lesson. Can't you just throw the ball to me so I can practice forehands?"

Or this:

"You call that wimpy, little swing a *forehand?* The ball came over the net like a mortally wounded duck in the middle of a long last dive."

"Well, Mr. DeWolf, my tennis teacher, told me to concentrate on hitting through the ball and not to worry too much about hitting it hard until I feel comfortable and confident with my swing."

"He did, huh? That sure doesn't sound right to me. Do you think I beat Hank Simpson every week by hitting powder-puff shots?"

"I don't know. I just . . ."

"Well, I don't. I put something on the ball from the forehand side. In fact most of the time I'm amazed that it doesn't just burn up before it gets to the net. Now I want you to do the same. This time, wind up and swing from the heels. Let's see some *pace.*"

Needless to say, this kind of "help" will only end up confusing and frustrating a child, and it certainly won't go over very well with the instructor. Yet it happens all the time. It is practically impossible to find a tennis teacher who has never experienced the unique thrill of sending a child home with the makings of some decent groundstrokes one day and having him come back without them the next.

"What happened to the strokes I taught you?" the instructor asks, even though the answer is obvious.

"My dad showed me how he does it."

"Right." (Sigh.)

"He's really a good player . . ."

"Right."

". . . and he says it looks like I will be just as good as him."

"So it seems. So it seems." (Heavy sigh.)

Practice with your child, but make sure you practice what the instructor has preached. Otherwise, you might as well forget about the kid ever receiving a solid foundation in the fundamentals of the game.

Before you can help your child practice, however, a competent tennis teacher must be located. But how do you go about finding one of those certified towers of tennis wisdom, one of those instructors adept at performing the delicate task of teaching this fairly complex physical skill to your very own flesh and blood?

If you belong to a tennis club, the resident pro is the logical candidate for the job. It should be easy enough to investigate his or her teaching methods. Talk to the pro yourself and solicit some testimonials from club members whose children have taken lessons there. If it sounds good and the price is right and your child is anxious to get started, sign 'em up.

If your "club" is the local municipal courts, the same basic procedure may be followed. Find someone who's familiar with the park's teaching pro and go from there.

In most cases, the municipal park pro will receive high marks from former students. The fact that incompetents usually don't last very long in either the clubs or the park systems is in your favor. But the free-lance ranks are loaded with "pros" who, to put it kindly, are totally unqualified, so be especially careful if you're in the market for a free-lancer.

There are several things to look for in determining whether any tennis instructor is good, bad, marginal, exceptional, or a plain and simple bummer. Playing ability is not one of them. That has very little to do with an instructor's ability to teach the game, except at the highly advanced level. Many successful professional players become teachers when their playing days are over and a lot of them are excellent at it. But winning Wimbledon, Forest Hills, or one of the other biggies doesn't automatically mean that the player will be able to teach a novice. Patience, a willingness to work hard, an ability to communicate, and a thorough understanding of the game are far more important than a roomful of tournament trophies and a winning smile when it comes to teaching.

Dennis Van der Meer, one of the top teaching professionals in the world, and the man whose expertise has proven invaluable to me and my game for many years, has never exactly been a slouch as a player, but his true genius lies in the area of teaching, not playing. When he realized that he lacked the necessary ability to reach the top as a player, his love of tennis prompted him to become a student of the game, and he quickly established himself as one of the best. Literally thousands of tennis players of all ages and skill levels have directly benefited from his insights and teaching methods.

But his influence reaches well beyond those people who have learned the game the Van der Meer way. He has lobbied long and hard for a system that will insure that *every* teaching pro is well qualified. It may well be impossible, but a bit of progress in that direction has already been made. Many teaching pros are members of a national organization of teaching professionals known as the United States Professional Teachers Association (USPTA). To qualify for membership, a teaching pro must pass a written test—which is fine as far as it goes, but it doesn't go quite far enough.

Passing such a test may demonstrate an individual's grasp of the subject, but several equally important attributes are left unmeasured: Will the instructor make the learning experience fun and enjoyable as well as productive? Will the instructor be astute enough to recognize the different needs of different students and imaginative or inventive enough to respond to those needs in a positive way? Will the instructor be able to motivate his or her students, young and old? To communicate with them? Will the students be excited with tennis, rather than turned off? Will they actually learn how to play the game?

If your child's potential tennis teacher rates a definite "yes" to each of the above questions, the kid will be in good hands. No doubt about it.

Although the parent and the tennis instructor are the two most influential factors in a child's ultimate development as a player, occasionally a child will survive both a demanding, insensitive parent and a thoroughly incompetent teacher and still enjoy playing the game.

But why take chances?

Tennis Camps

"What did you do on your vacation?"

"I took a tennis lesson."

"A tennis lesson? Just one?"

"Yep."

"For two weeks?"

"Yeah. I went to a tennis camp."

To be fair, a tennis camp session isn't exactly a marathon lesson, but it's awfully close. The tennis camper will spend a lot of time on the court during the day and will usually pass the evening hours sitting with fellow campers around an empty tennis court instead of a campfire, swapping not ghost stories, but tennis stories. (Most tennis stories are scarier than ghost stories anyway.)

Yes, the immersion in the sport is just about total at a tennis camp.

Though only about six dozen such camps were operating in the United States a decade ago, approximately ten times that number are in existence today, and new ones are popping up daily.

The rapid growth of this industry is yet another reflection of tennis' surging popularity and one that provides an extremely beneficial service to thousands of tennis players, including a number of playing pros who occasionally spend time at a camp re-educating themselves in the fundamentals.

No matter what a tennis player might need—schooling in the basics or just re-sharpening the edges of a game dulled from neglect—there's definitely a tennis camp somewhere that is ready, willing, and able to help out.

Tennis camps, not surprisingly, range from the incredibly plush and luxurious to the strictly spartan, no-frills type. But they all promise prospective clients one thing: tennis and lots of it.

There are camps for adults, camps for children, and camps for the entire family. At a family institution, Mom and Dad may spend some time going through an intensive refresher course while the talented teen is off being videotaped for an in-depth stroke analysis and the nine-year-old neophyte is learning how to grip the racquet in a beginner's class. Meanwhile, the most recent addition to the family roster is safely ensconced in a day-care center near the courts trying desperately to figure out what's causing all those funny "plopping" sounds outside.

Sounds idyllic, doesn't it. Well, it can be, but only if you happen to select a well-run tennis camp. If you commit your family to a fly-by-night, take-the-money-and-run outfit, however, the tennis camp experience will become a nightmare.

So it is with children's, or junior, camps. And I would think twice about sending a child with hardly any tennis background to a one- or two-week session at a tennis camp, regardless of how good the camp might be. That would be taking too much of a chance of tennis overkill. If, however, the child has demonstrated a consistently strong interest in tennis, a camp can be a sound investment and a lot of fun. Junior camps offer the same basic benefits as do group lessons. The young player will develop with others and there will be plenty of available playing and practice partners of equal or superior ability.

Locating the right camp for your child is similar to shopping for the right racquet or the right instructor: Know exactly what you're looking for and go out and find it. The local club or tennis shop should be able to provide you with a complete list of camps in your area. Write to several of the camps asking for information concerning their programs.

Here are a few things to look for:

Cost Tennis camps are not inexpensive. You can expect to pay between $200 and $350 per week, but if the camp is a good one, and you can afford it, the money will be well spent.

Housing Remember that you're sending your child to a tennis camp, not a prison camp. He or she certainly won't need a private suite with a queen size waterbed and thick-pile shag carpeting on the floor, but does deserve something more than an army cot. After all, it's not supposed to be a boot camp either. The less expensive camps usually provide dormitory-type housing (many camps are conducted on college campuses during the summer when the students are away), and that arrangement will be more than adequate.

Non-tennis facilities Swimming pools, saunas, game rooms, and polo fields are not vital, but many tennis camps offer a few non-tennis recreational outlets. They can definitely contribute to a child's overall enjoyment of the camp experience. Of course there's always a possibility that you'll send off a future Wimbledon champ and welcome home a pinball wizard.

Tennis facilities Find out how many courts the camp has and how many students will be attending with your child.

Now, armed with these two numbers, do a little simple arithmetic. If, for example, there are two tennis courts for every hundred or so campers, it is advisable to look for a camp with a better court/kid ratio—eight players to six courts is a reasonable number. Mechanical aids, such as videotape equipment (used for stroke analysis) and ball machines can enhance the learning experience and should be included on the plus side of the ledger.

Teaching staff Again, the first thing to check out is the instructor/pupil ratio. Too few instructors will usually result

99

in impersonal and, therefore, ineffective instruction. Also make sure there is sufficient on-site personnel to deal with any camper insurrections. Find out if the teaching staff is properly supervised, organized, and qualified to teach. It's extremely important that the teaching staff adheres to a common pattern of instruction. Since the young campers will have contact with several different instructors during the camp session, a consistent teaching system will be less confusing and more effective.

Once you have found a tennis camp that seems to meet these requirements, you should sit down with the potential camper before mailing off the deposit. Since the camp will require substantial investments of your money and your child's time and effort, both of you should be fully aware of what you're getting into.

If, after the facts are laid out, the child still expresses a strong desire to attend and you are convinced that desire is sincere, it's time to get the suitcase out of the attic.

Practice

As we all know, practice makes perfect, right? Not in tennis it doesn't. If it did, I should have played at least one perfect match by now. Or one perfect game. But I haven't, and I never will. In fact, I'm still waiting to hit a perfect shot. I've hit a few that were *almost* perfect, but so far absolute perfection has eluded me and every other tennis player.

Tennis does not have an equivalent of golf's hole-in-one, bowling's 300, or baseball's perfect game. Rather, it is a sport in which even the best players can, and do, make the same mistake not just twice, but hundreds of times.

One of the most appealing aspects of the game, at least for me, is that there are no upper limits on the level of per-

100

formance. No matter how good a person becomes, there is still room for improvement. Tennis may be easily learned, but it is never mastered.

So practice won't make a player perfect, but it will make a player better.

And to give you an idea of just how important practice is to a tennis player, it is not unusual for a professional player to shower and change into fresh tennis clothes and spend a couple of hours on the practice court almost immediately after playing a tournament match.

I can't even begin to guess how many hours I've spent working out for every hour I've spent in actual competition, but it's got to be well into the thousands. Fortunately, I love tennis so much that practicing has never been a chore for me. That doesn't mean it isn't hard work, though. It's just that it is hard work I happen to find enjoyable.

That's the key to practice, especially for a child. It must be fun. If it's not, the child should hang up the racquet and look for something that is.

Though my enjoyment of tennis practice was spontaneous and totally natural, some children may require the interjection of a planned element of fun into the proceedings.

An effective and productive practice session consists primarily of periods of repetition, which is only normal. Parents who plan to function as their offspring's live-in practice partners must, therefore, be sensitive to the child's emotional needs as well as his or her tennis needs during a practice session. A parent who fails to recognize the former or, worse yet, ignores them, may well end up sitting across the dinner table from an ex-player.

Let's assume that your child has just completed a lesson and is anxious to get back on the court to practice the day's subject matter, the serve. You've been thinking about taking a look at the vacuum cleaner that has suddenly developed a tendency to exhale instead of inhale, but when your child approaches you with fire in his eyes and a racquet in his hot little hands, you immediately decide that spending time with him is more important than getting a few dog hairs off the living room carpet.

A short time later you're on the court warming up and feeling pretty smug because you actually remembered to bring along the old diaper pail that now serves as a container for the several dozen practice balls you've accumulated. You also feel a brief twinge of sadness when you realize that it was only yesterday that the little person on the other side of the net was filling the diaper pail with diapers instead of tennis balls.

"Ready?"

"Any time you are."

"Okay. But I'm not very good at serving. That's why I wanted to practice."

"I'm sure you'll do just fine."

And he does, every once in a while. But you notice that he's throwing the ball way out in front and far to the side pretty consistently.

"Looks like you're having some trouble with the toss."

"Yeah, I know what I'm supposed to do, but sometimes I forget about doing it."

"Hey, I know the feeling."

Suddenly the serves are coming in fairly regularly.

"That was a real beauty. Looks like you're getting your toss problem licked."

Before long, the child begins to look a bit weary.

"Are you getting tired?"

"A little. But I'd like to hit a few more, and then work on my forehand for a while."

"Fine. Let's spend another five minutes with the serve, and then fifteen minutes on your forehand. But now that you're serving so well, why don't we work on your accuracy? I brought along a couple of empty ball cans we can use as targets."

"Great idea. That sounds like fun."

He hits a few dozen serves at the makeshift targets that you set up around the service court and he even scores a couple of direct hits.

"Dad, all that serving kind of wore me out. Do you mind if we skip the forehand workout?"

"Not at all. Besides, if you hit forehand as well as you serve, I'd have a hard time keeping up with you."

"I had a lot of fun. Can we do it again? Soon?"

"You bet."

And you walk off the court feeling good and planning for the next time. Alright!!

You've proven that happy endings aren't necessarily restricted to fairy tales and Gidget movies, and you, the parent, are entitled to take a bow for a job well done. You were on the ball from the word go, and you didn't even come close to falling off.

Unfortunately, not every parent is as intelligent and sensitive as you.

Take that other father/son duo that was a couple of courts down from you. Things turned out quite a bit differently for them. They too came to practice, and if you'd happened to glance in their direction, it would have appeared that all was well. A closer look, however, would have revealed that something vital was missing from their practice session: an element of fun. You would have seen that neither father nor son was smiling. In fact, the child looked as if he'd rather be anywhere but on that tennis court. Like home reading a book, which is exactly what he'd been doing before his father came in and told him to put down the book and pick up his racquet.

"Do I have to, Dad? I really don't feel much like practicing right now."

"What do you mean, 'Do I have to?' I thought you wanted to be a tennis player."

"Not exactly. I just want to play tennis. You know, for fun."

"Sure, sure. But do you think Jimmy Connors and Bjorn Borg got where they are by sitting around reading books? Not on your life they didn't. They got where they are by playing tennis, by practicing. I bet they practiced at least an hour a day when they were your age."

"But I don't want to be Jimmy Connors or Bjorn Borg. I just wanna be me."

"Cut out the Sammy Davis, Jr., imitation and get your racquet."

Obviously, the child had no choice but to give in and hope for the best. He didn't get it though, not by a long shot. If you'd been paying attention to them instead of having so much fun with your own child, this is what you would have seen and heard:

"Okay, Son. I want you to hit some serves. Let's go." The child, whose age, size, and tennis ability mirrored that of your own child's, unenthusiastically began hitting serves while his father very enthusiastically jumped on the successful ones and belted them back across the net. Naturally the child's concentration and rhythm were disturbed because he was afraid of getting nailed by one of the scorching returns. He soon faltered, and the father immediately got ticked off.

"Who taught you how to serve, your mother? You're tossing the ball all over the sky. I've seen better swings on a broken-down playground. C'mon, shape up. And try to hit them down the middle, will you? I want to practice my backhand return."

"Dad, can we quit now? My arm's really tired."

"Quit? We just got started. How can your arm be tired already? Just keep serving to my backhand side and forget about hitting the service court. We only have the court for another forty-five minutes or so, and I want you to try to get the ball over the net every now and again. I'm doing this for you, and don't you forget it."

Who can blame the poor kid for dreaming about joining the French Foreign Legion at the first available opportunity?

It doesn't take a genius to figure out that our hypothetical Simon Legree violated every conceivable rule in the book of how to be an effective practice partner.

Things got off to a bad start when the unfortunate child was *forced* to practice after coming right out and saying he didn't feel like it. The demanding parent wasn't out of line in suggesting a practice session, but the matter should have been dropped when the child declined the invitation. Your child, on the other hand, approached you with a request to go out and play. Since you were in a position to comply, it worked out nicely. That doesn't mean a parent must drop whatever he or she is doing if the child expresses a desire to go hit a few though. Parents should not put themselves at the mercy of their children's spontaneous desires to play tennis, but when it's right, go for it!

Our hypothetical example of what not to do certainly swung into high gear when he finally got his reluctant child onto the court. Surely you noticed that the child had nothing to say about *what* segment of his game he wanted to work on; the parent made that arbitrary decision. As a result, the trip to the court became a practice session for the father rather than the son. There's nothing wrong with that, provided of course that all involved are aware of the session's goal. In this case, however, the parent dragged the child out to the court under somewhat false pretenses. If the father wanted to practice his backhand service return, he should have said so at the outset. It's quite possible that the child may have been willing to go along under those conditions.

Meanwhile, you wisely let your child determine the content of *his* practice session. You were bright enough to realize that creaming his serve attempts might unnecessarily unnerve him, so you confined yourself to catching the balls and watching his form for obvious flaws. Not so with Mr. Gung-Ho. He

106

couldn't resist the opportunity to destroy his child's confidence by practically jamming his son's efforts right back down his throat. He also couldn't resist letting the child know that his serves left something to be desired. There's nothing like an insult or two to build morale.

Instead of insults, you chose to gently call attention to the fact that your child's service toss was slightly out of sync. Not surprisingly, he was aware of the problem and he quickly let you know that he was working on getting it together. Your show of understanding and your emphasis on his accomplishments and progress was exactly right.

So, for that matter, was your suggestion of using the empty tennis ball cans as aids in an accuracy drill. The cans, of course, provided your child with a highly visible measurement of his successful attempts to hit serves to different areas of the service court, and they broke up the tedium of serving ball after ball.

The parent in the second scenario also tried to introduce an accuracy test into the proceedings, but he choose a less than productive means of doing so.

Finally, you offered no protest when your child decided he'd had enough for the day. Knowing when to quit is an extremely important part of a successful practice session. Insisting that your child continue after he or she has lost interest could easily be the beginning of a permanent loss of interest in the game.

To summarize, the cardinal rules of practicing with a child are:

1. Be sure the child wants to practice. Don't use force.
2. Be patient. Practicing with a beginner will require a lot of patience.
3. Go slowly. A good practice session means a lot of

repetition, and a beginner won't make much progress if you decide to move onto something else after hitting only a couple of serves, forehands, etc.

4. Plan the practice session. Decide exactly what stroke or strokes are going to be emphasized and stick to those. Of course, you should make sure the session doesn't conflict with what the child is learning in his or her lessons or *how* the child is learning it. Practice should complement the lessons, not supplant them.

5. Tailor the practice to the child, taking into account such factors as age, size, and stamina. An effective way of doing this is to utilize time limits rather than a specific number of repetitions. In other words, allot fifteen minutes for backhand practice instead of asking for a hundred backhands.

6. Emphasize accomplishments and progress, not mistakes.

7. Introduce an element of fun. You can do this without putting on clown makeup and pratfalling all over the court.

8. Stop at the first sign of disinterest.

As the child's skill level increases, practice sessions can be enlivened by utilizing a series of preplanned drills. For instance, you might place a towel in each corner of the backcourt as targets and have the child hit forehands at them from the baseline. Or you might consider incorporating a bit of cooperative competition. Instead of saying, "Why don't we work on your forehand for a while," say, "Do you think you can hit ten forehands without missing?" Just keep in mind: To be effective a practice drill must stress repetition.

Once the child has a good grasp of the fundamentals of tennis, a certain amount of practice time should be devoted to simulating actual playing conditions. Arrange a set sequence of shots and play them over and over. Let's say you want to practice your service return and the child wants to practice crosscourt forehands. No problem. Have the child serve the ball and you hit the returns down the line to the forehand side. The child then hits his crosscourt forehands. Obviously, the possible shot sequences are infinite so it shouldn't be difficult to find a combination that will enable both of you to work on different aspects of your games at the same time. The practice will then be mutually beneficial and what could be better than that?

Practicing with another player isn't always possible, however, and that's when a backboard comes in handy. Solitary practice against a wall or backboard can be extremely beneficial and a lot of fun if it's done properly.

The most common mistake children make when hitting against a wall is trying to kill the ball. This tendency to sacrifice form for power can be damaging and it takes a certain amount of restraint to play the wall or backboard advantageously. The child should learn to stand well back from the wall and not worry about making contact on the first bounce. Trying to hit the ball on a single bounce will result in hurried, unnatural strokes. Since it travels only half as far as it would on a tennis court, the ball comes back twice as quickly so adjustments have to be made.

A backboard is an excellent device for grooving groundstrokes or practicing serves. It helps if, on the board, there is a clearly marked line approximating the net as a visual reference point. No matter how technically perfect a stroke might be, it's absolutely worthless if the ball's trajectory is consistently six inches lower than the net height.

No tennis player ever outgrows the need for practice, so the child whose early practice experiences are pleasant and productive will be well on the way toward making the sport a permanent part of his or her life.

Family Play

There are several ways of making a family match competitively even without sacrificing anyone's enjoyment of the outing. The family hot-shot may have to cool it somewhat, but toning down a game to keep the ball in play against a weaker player can be as challenging as trying to put it away against a player of comparable skill. In any event, there's no joy whatever in steamrolling over an opponent who has a much lower skill level. When that happens no one really wins.

Every tennis player knows that the quickest way to improve is to play against opponents of equal or superior ability, but occasionally hitting against a weaker player will not harm anyone's game.

If the parents are better players than their offspring the obvious answer for evening up a family doubles match is to make sure the strong players are on opposite sides of the net. Finding a reasonably competitive family lineup will require some experimentation and may result in some strange alignments, but that shouldn't be an inhibiting factor. If Mom and Dad find themselves facing their twelve-year-old twin daughters, or if you end up with a men's doubles team against a women's doubles team, don't worry about it. No one's going to report you to the United States Tennis Association. The main goal is to make sure everyone in the family derives the maximum amount of enjoyment from the outing.

If necessary, additional compensations in the interest of equal competition can become a part of the match. Probably the most effective equalizer is spotting the weaker player or players one or two points per game. This is also a common practice in singles matches featuring players of uneven abilities.

Restricting the area of the court a stronger player has to cover is another good equalizer. Many matches that would normally be complete routs have been made extremely close by opening up the doubles alleys to the less skilled player, while confining the better player to the singles court. The same results may also be obtained by allowing a strong player only one serve instead of two.

Structuring the game to meet your family's needs, however, won't do much good unless you have a place to put the system to the test. Unless you happen to own your own court or have a very, very good friend who owns one, your first order of business will be finding a place to play.

There are basically four options open to you if you don't own a court or have access to someone else's.

You can build one, of course, but that's not always the most practical solution, especially if you live in an apartment or on rented property. Besides, having a tennis court installed can cost about as much as a college education.

The second option is also fairly expensive, but it's one that an increasing number of families are taking advantage of. Surely there's at least one tennis club near your home by now. Like the aforementioned tennis camps, these private clubs are springing up all over the place and one of them just might solve your problem. In fact, if you live in an area that tends to have a few inches of white stuff on the ground for a few months a year, and if your family is really hooked on tennis, a club membership may be almost a necessity. Many clubs have both indoor and outdoor courts, a staff of personnel that includes qualified instructors, and a family membership program. Some clubs have facilities for racquetball as well as tennis, and several of them provide their members with everything from

111

pro shops to exercise rooms to coffee shops and bars.

Before you rush out to sign up, however, check the club out very carefully. Visit the facilities and talk to some of the members before you make the decision to join. Does the club offer a program for each member of the family? Are junior players severely restricted by the hours in which they're allowed to play? Are there court fees that are charged over and above the monthly dues? How far in advance must a court be reserved? Three hours? Three days? Three weeks? Find out before you take the plunge or you may regret the fact you ever heard of tennis.

Initial membership fees and monthly dues vary from club to club, but if you're satisfied that a particular establishment will adequately meet your family's needs and you can afford it, then by all means go ahead and join.

If putting a tennis court in the backyard or joining a tennis club is geographically impossible or financially impractical, however, don't despair. There is another alternative and it costs very little or nothing at all.

I'm referring, of course, to the public courts. Ah, the public courts. How well I know the trials and tribulations, the frustrations and agonies, the poignant little human dramas that occur in and around those chain link enclosures.

I grew up on the public courts in Long Beach and I spent countless hours clinging to the fence separating me from the already occupied object of my pursuit: the tennis court.

I used to get really steamed when I was hanging around waiting for a court while the adults therein would play for a couple of hours and then decide to play "one more quick set." I found myself at the mercy of these "court hogs" often enough to have vowed that when I became an adult, I would give kids equal time.

About the closest I ever came to having a case of hero

worship was when two men who were regulars at Houghton Park would invite Jerry Cromwell and me to play doubles with them. They didn't even seem to mind if we won, but they were the exception. Nobody else would even give us the time of day and more than once our ultimately fruitless tennis court vigils lasted a full eight hours.

If anything, the situation is even worse today. But, of course, you've already discovered that for yourself. Whenever you decide to take the family over to the park to play and hit the ball for a while, it seems as if thirty-nine million of the forty million tennis players in the country all live in your neighborhood and all of them want to play when you do.

The fact that most of our public tennis facilities are over-crowded is frustrating to many adults who squeeze their playing time into a schedule that's already stretched to the limit by work and family obligations, but it's just as bad for children. In fact, it may even be worse for youngsters, especially if they're not very good players.

I've seen many instances when children have patiently waited for an open court only to find themselves subjected to a steady stream of verbal abuse from adults who feel the youngsters have no business on the court.

The reasoning goes something like this: "I work hard for a living and I have to play tennis to relax. Besides, my taxes pay for this court so I should have priority over these snotty-nosed kids who can't even get a decent rally going."

Well, I've got news for you. As long as the children observe the rules and regulations that are in effect concerning the use of the court, they have as much right to play tennis there as anyone else.

Because I feel so strongly about the right of children to play tennis, I am extremely concerned about the fact that some municipal park administrators have decided to charge court fees at municipal facilities. So far, there are only a few isolated instances of this, but the fact that it's happening at all is outrageous. And particularly distressing is the fact that a fee is now being charged on the courts in Long Beach where I first learned the game. A dollar an hour isn't an exorbitant sum of money for an hour of tennis, but that's not the point. Charging *any* fee, no matter how nominal, automatically excludes a huge number of children from playing, and that is grossly unfair.

If I had to pay a buck for every hour I spent on a municipal tennis court when I was young, I'd be paying off the debt for the rest of my life. Actually, I never would have become a tennis player at all if I'd had to shell out a buck an hour.

What it all boils down to is that there weren't enough public tennis courts twenty-five years ago, and there aren't enough today. And since the players whose only outlet is the public courts are in pretty much the same boat, the best you and your family can hope for is that everyone who frequents your favorite tennis court scrupulously observes the time limit that is posted on the fence. Other than that, I can only offer my sympathy with your plight and remind you to keep in mind that patience is supposed to be a virtue.

When I began discussing where you and your family can play tennis, I said there were four primary options open to you. So far, three of those options have been examined; I'm somewhat hesitant to unveil number four because I don't recommend it. In the interest of thorough treatment of the "where-to-play problem," however, I will reluctantly present your final alternative. It's simply: You can give up tennis altogether. Or, in the case of an entire family, all together. But that would be a terrible mistake, so don't even think about it.

Instead, let's assume that you and your family have decided to become regular visitors at the public courts down the street. And let's further assume that you have developed an effective, mutually agreeable handicapping system that is guaranteed to make the weekly family doubles match enjoyable for each participant. So far, so good.

But . . . if you aren't already aware of the fact that tennis has been known to put a strain on interfamily relationships, it's time you learned about that singularly sinister side of the sport right now.

For some reason, the gentle game of tennis often brings out the worst in some people. Anyone who has spent any time around a tennis court has undoubtedly witnessed at least one gruesome instance of a husband mercilessly berating his wife for messing up an easy shot during a "friendly" game of mixed doubles. I use the example of a husband blasting a wife because it rarely happens the other way around. And for some strange reason such behavior seems to occur solely among members of the same family. You will seldom, if ever, see some guy jump all over his buddy during a match, no matter how many shots the buddy butchers. But put Mr. Sweetness and Light and his wife on the same side of the net and watch the fireworks fly. I'm not sure I know why it's so easy to criticize a husband, wife, or child on the tennis court, but it happens quite frequently. And I must admit that for many years my husband Larry refused to play tennis with me because he claimed I hogged the ball and couldn't resist pointing out his errors. Now I'm not about to admit that he was right, but our problem is now a thing of the past, and we play together without friction. I only mention it to illustrate that tennis can affect even the most easygoing, compatible off-court relationships. Fortunately, however, we never quite reached the insult-trading, shouting stage, but many family duos do.

Such verbal assaults are totally uncalled for and distasteful when mature adults are involved, but when a child is on the receiving end of a parental rampage because the kid did something as inconsequential as hitting a tennis ball into the net, it is positively revolting. A parent who verbally abuses a child on the tennis court for making a mistake is completely beneath contempt.

Tennis can provide you and your family with many hours of enjoyment and togetherness if you let it. But be careful that you don't allow a mere game to harm something as precious as your relationship with someone you love. Doing so is both stupid and pointless.

9

The Mental Game

At the highest levels of tennis competition the physical skills of the players are extremely close. As a result, the player who eventually triumphs is generally the one who is better prepared mentally. But at any level of play, tennis requires players to use their heads and to be mentally alert.

Tennis players have more than a few things to think about. They must think about the ball, about distances and angles, about the net, about their opponent, about their swing, about the wind if they're playing outdoors and the artificial lighting if they're playing indoors, about their position on the court, about the score, and a thousand other things.

But tennis is not unique in this regard. Every sport demands a certain amount of mental involvement from its participants.

The term "psyching up" has worked its way into our sports lexicon, and the constant reference to this term by athletes in all sports indicates just how important mental preparation can be.

"Getting up for the game" is another term that has been added to the growing list of sports clichés. It doesn't mean climbing out of the sack and heading for the stadium, field, or court—as a literal interpretation may suggest. Getting up for the game is just another way of saying psyching up or "Well, the ol' bod's ready to perform . . . if the mind can get it together and carry its share of the burden."

But no matter how it's said, an athlete's state of mind affects physical performance, so the young tennis player should begin by trying to focus his or her thoughts on the task at hand—playing tennis.

I always try to spend several minutes before a match or practice session thinking about what I'm going to do on the court, and I've found that putting everything but tennis out of my mind can often has a positive effect on my performance. Of course, it's not always easy to banish potentially disrupting thoughts from my mind and sometimes it's impossible, but I always make the effort.

Obviously, it's better to think positively during a pre-tennis period of mental exercise, but children should be cautioned against thinking unrealistically. If they do, disappointment is bound to follow. Positive visualization carries no guarantee that things will turn out the way they are imagined, but *negative* visualization has a definite tendency to be reinforced by the actual performance. If a child is convinced that his serve is going to let him down during a match, nine times out of ten it will. But if he says to himself "My serve has been giving me some trouble recently, so instead of trying to hit aces I'm just going to concentrate on getting the ball into play," the odds of having the troublesome serve come around are definitely in his favor.

Court Sense

Court sense does *not* refer to the uncanny knack of arriving at the local public courts just as a vacancy occurs. Though

118

that is an extremely valuable and useful trait, it's definitely something about which I am unable to offer any thoughts other than to say some people have it and some don't. The court sense I mean is something that manifests itself once a vacant court has been located and subsequently occupied.

I'm referring, of course, to that sixth sense, that instinct with which certain players have been blessed. It is a form of human radar that occurs when an innate understanding of angles and an ability to quickly compute and translate that understanding into a physical reaction are combined. In simpler terms, a player who is somehow able to consistently anticipate an opponent's shots has court sense, while a player who is seldom able to maneuver into a position to effectively return an opponent's shots doesn't. The players who possess court sense are easily identified: They're the ones who are almost always in the right place at the right time. And, like the mysterious power that enables some people to stumble across available courts, some players have court sense and some don't.

Fortunately, most tennis players have at least some degree of court sense. The players at the very top, however, have it flowing through their veins. They automatically know exactly where they are on the court, and they are incredibly adept at putting themselves in a position of being able to cover the maximum amount of court area with a minimum amount of effort.

Of course, no one has a court sense that's so finely honed that it never fails them. The tennis player hasn't been born yet who can correctly anticipate every shot, every time.

If you think that court sense is a difficult aspect of the game to teach, you're absolutely right. It can, however, be cultivated and refined.

To determine if their children are among the lucky ones, parents should carefully watch them, paying special attention to whether or not the kids demonstrate a tendency to know where the ball is going to land before their opponent hits it. If they seem to display a definite "feel" in this area, they do indeed have a healthy amount of court sense.

But if your child seems to be lost in the wilderness, do not despair, there's still hope. The first thing to do is sit down with the child and explain the principles of deductive reasoning. It's a good idea to augment the lecture with simple diagrams illustrating how it is possible to place the ball in an area of the court where your opponent's choice of returns will be limited. Theoretically, the diagrams should show the child that he or she can sometimes influence the angle of return which, of course, will work to his or her advantage. Go easy on these chalkboard sessions though. It won't exactly fire up the child if his tennis education becomes a blizzard of graph paper, geometric theorems, and slide rule calculations. The sessions should be limited to helping the child *visualize* the concept of court sense.

On-court demonstrations can be even more effective at this than diagrams. Here's how it works:

Stand about three feet outside the sideline and halfway between the baseline and the net, or about where you'd have to be to return a sharply angled crosscourt shot. Now, ask your child to stand on the spot which he or she thinks is the optimum position to return your most logical shot. If the child immediately comes over to your side of the net and stands behind you, you're probably being insulted in mime. If the child immediately goes over and sits on the bench next to the court, it's a good bet that you have a ways to go before he or she understands what you're trying to do.

But chances are the child will figure out that your ability to hit a successful shot from outside the court is definitely limited by the angle from which you must hit it.

And maybe the child'll even pick up on the fact that

where he or she stands can further decrease your placement options. Staging several similar situations and hitting a lot of balls from each should give your child a good grasp of the principles of court sense. Whether or not the child is able to adjust to the situations that occur during game conditions, however, is beyond your powers of instruction.

By far the best way to work on your child's court sense is to play a lot of tennis together. With experience comes wisdom, and with wisdom comes a certain amount of court sense . . . sometimes.

121

Concentration

Of all the component parts which make up this game called tennis, concentration—the ability to focus one's attention on the ball, the object in play—is the single most important. A child may possess the classiest strokes imaginable, but if he or she either lacks concentration totally or is unable to sustain it for any length of time, those strokes will end up being technically perfect whiffs as often as not.

After all, the ball has to be *seen* to be hit with anything resembling consistency, and concentration in tennis on a basic level simply means keeping the ball in sight. Of course, the person on the other side of the net shouldn't be ignored completely, but a child should learn to play the ball, not the opponent.

It sounds simple enough, but in reality learning to really see the ball is definitely one of the most difficult tasks any tennis player faces. And it's doubly hard for younger children because most of them have fleeting attention spans—except, of course, when the Saturday morning cartoon festivals keep them riveted to the tube.

Teaching a child to concentrate on the court isn't the easiest thing in the world to do, but it's not imposible either. Actually, it might be more correct to say that the ability to concentrate is acquired rather than learned because there are a million and one things that can disrupt concentration and most of them have no relation to the game of tennis. A silence-shattering siren, a sudden sonic boom, or an earthquake are examples of concentration busters, but most disruptions are more subtle than those. Anything that causes a tennis player to forget the ball for even a fraction of a second is an enemy of concentration. But it is the mind itself that is the primary villain.

122

There have been plenty of times when I was playing an important match and suddenly realized that my mind had wandered somewhere else and I wasn't watching the ball properly. It's always been a constant struggle for me to maintain a high degree of vigilance, a struggle that requires a tremendous amount of effort and conscious thought.

But the most ironic thing about a concentration lapse is that you may not even be aware it's happening. You may think you are focusing on the ball, even when you're not.

By focusing on "the third party in the match," I mean becoming totally involved with it every second it's in play. When I'm playing well, it's usually because my involvement with the ball is complete. I see it from the moment it leaves my opponent's racquet face until it's sitting on the strings of *my* racquet and at every point in between. At such times, I'm so sensitive to the ball that I can actually see the direction in

which it's spinning before it crosses the net into my territory. The ball appears to be bigger and moving slower than it really is when I'm concentrating. But if it looks like an aspirin tablet when it comes rocketing across the net, I know I'm in big deep trouble.

Attaining the ability the really see the ball, however, depends mostly on individual mental discipline. Still, there are a few things a parent can do to help a child in this area besides saying "Watch the ball" every few minutes. Reminding the child to keep his or her peepers on the sphere is a good idea, as long as you don't go overboard and end up sounding more naggy than helpful. Besides, the child already *knows* that watching the ball is important. It's doing it that's difficult.

Since seeing the ball is the ultimate goal, it stands to reason that making the ball easier to see is a good first step. This can be accomplished by using high-visibility yellow balls when playing or practicing with your child. Yellow balls are much easier to see than are, say, white ones. Though most tournaments now use yellow balls, Wimbledon still uses white, and I have a problem seeing them well after playing with yellow ones most of the time.

Using a high-visibility ball is a good beginning, but you can take it one step further. If the balls are fairly new, tell the child to watch the manufacturer's logo while the ball is in flight. If the balls are pretty well worn, take a felt pen and mark them with your own clever logo; better yet, let your child draw a little something on the surface of the ball.

The point is to get some sort of visible target on which the child can focus. Trying to see the ball is one thing, but trying to see something *on* the ball will intensify the effort. After that, there's not a whole lot you can do except hope that the child truly comes to understand the correlation between seeing the ball and hitting it successfully.

124

Seeing the flight of the ball, however, is only one battle in the war to achieve a high degree of concentration.

Hearing the ball is also extremely important. Sound crazy? Well, it's not. Tuning in to the sound of the ball in flight can tell a player a great deal about the ball's speed, or pace, and spin. Listening to the ball meet your opponent's racquet can reveal the same vital information—how fast it is coming and how much spin has been applied.

The benefits of hearing the ball are best appreciated when a situation exists where the sound is missing. For instance, if a low-flying jet passes over a court at the moment a player is serving, thereby obliterating the sound of the serve, the receiver will have an extremely difficult time judging the speed of the ball.

Although it sounds impossible, there is at least one player who relies totally on her sense of hearing to play tennis. Though blind since the age of four-and-a-half, Chris Ehler began playing when she was a sixteen-year-old high school junior. At first she spent several hours a day practicing against a backboard using special balls implanted with tiny bells. By concentrating on the *sound* of the object she couldn't see, Chris soon reached the point where she felt she was ready for actual competition. Though she didn't fare too well at first, she quickly began to hold her own against her disbelieving sighted friends.

After a year of playing with the "tinkle balls," she gave them up and began using regular balls. With the acute hearing that blind people develop to compensate for their lack of sight, she was able to play a credible game of tennis merely by focusing on the sound of the ball. It's almost frightening to imagine what Chris Ehler could do on the tennis court if she could see the ball.

If watching the ball and listening to it are the main ingredients in the recipe for concentration, racquet awareness is the frosting.

As a child becomes more proficient on the court, he or she should learn to be aware of the position of the racquet face in relation to the ball at all times. Highly skilled players know where their racquets are at all times, but many players, including practically every beginner, often don't have a clue. They may think the racquet is at shoulder level when it's actually down around around the ankles somewhere. The result: many swings and quite a few misses. A sense of racquet awareness is attained through constant feedback, experience, and imagining where it should be on any given stroke.

126

Strategy: Singles Play

Since a tennis player's main objective is to outwit the opponent, the first rule of strategy is to become acquainted with your own game. An intimate knowledge of your own strengths and weaknesses is absolutely vital.

The second rule of strategy is to be aware of your opponent's strengths and weaknesses.

All other things being equal, the player who is able to utilize his or her own strengths while negating those of the person on the other side of the net will usually win the match. And unless you play against the same opponents on a fairly regular basis, determining what to do on the court will rest on your ability to analyze the unfamiliar opposition's game quickly and accurately.

When I'm playing a tournament or World Team Tennis match, I'm usually very familiar with my opponent's game from past experience. But if I have to go against someone I've never seen before, I try to talk to a few players who can tell me what to expect. If, for example, it turns out that my opponent is deadly from the baseline but doesn't move well to the net, you can bet that I'll try to turn the court into Drop Shot City when I get out there. Or if the player isn't particularly fond of long rallies, I'll stand there and hit the ball all day.

But, as we all know, even the best laid plans can go astray. Maybe the baseline whiz who usually can't run down a good drop shot to save her life will suddenly start handling mine with ease. Or maybe my drop shot will have gone on vacation without notifying me. What then? Well, unless I have something else up my sleeve, I'm going to get demolished.

For that reason, I always approach a match with at least four or five alternative game plans. If one tactic goes haywire, there's another one waiting in the wings; if they all go haywire and I'm down 0–5, it's probably just not my day.

Some players, however, are unable to diversify on the court because they have locked themselves into a single pattern of play. Quite often, such players are lost if their game is getting picked apart by an opponent because they don't have the confidence or ability to abandon their bread and butter style of play.

Chris Evert, for example, has a reputation as a conservative baseline player. Actually, she is an *aggressive* baseline player. She can stand back there for hours hitting flat groundstrokes to one corner and then the other while literally running her opponent into the ground. Though she's developed a very respectable net game, Chris is so good at her particular style of play, she doesn't usually spend a lot of time worrying about elaborate strategies. That is left to her opponents, who have tried just about every tactic imaginable except locking her in a closet. But through it all, Chris Evert wins an awful lot of tennis matches.

So it is not particularly surprising that many young players, especially girls, are emulating the Evert style. There's absolutely nothing wrong with a conservative baseline game. In fact, players who become proficient at it generally have a lower mistake ratio than the more aggressive player. Besides, the game of tennis is built on the baseline player's most effective weapon: the groundstrokes. Though it's not my normal style of play by any means, there have been times when I've played matches from the baseline, and I must say it can be a lot of fun. Making it a steady diet, however, would drive me crazy because conservative play definitely conflicts with my nature.

I have always gravitated toward the all-court style of play, and I would recommend that children who are learning tennis do the same. An all-court game will give the child a valuable strategic weapon: flexibility. But beyond that, it demands a tremendous amount of involvement in the game by offering more opportunity to be creative and to move.

There is one more basic style of play that lies somewhere between the baseline and the all-court games. The serve-and-volley is favored, naturally enough, by players who have a strong serve. Though in some people's minds I am a serve-and-volley player, that style of play doesn't particularly turn me on because the points rarely last more than a few seconds. The server unleashes a boomer and follows it to the net and waits for a weak service return to wobble back across the net. Then, boom, the ball is put away with a winning volley and it's time to do it again. The serve-and-volley player is most effective on fast surfaces, but if the opponent's specialty happens to be the *return* of service, the hit-and-run player might as well be

playing against a backboard. Unless, of course, he or she has some decent groundstrokes and the sense to make a few adjustments.

Personally, I don't think children should restrict themselves to a serve-and-volley game, especially if they tend to reach the net before their serves. I do, however, believe that making the serve-and-volley a tactic in their overall game is a good idea.

A parent should *never* force a particular style of play on a child. If the kid likes to fly all over the court, or to stay back at the baseline, fine. Let him do it. The child must be comfortable on the court to derive pleasure from the game.

But regardless of which style of play young tennis players evolve, it is imperative that they learn to capitalize on their strengths, but not to the point where weak spots are ignored. Just because a child has a dynamite forehand it doesn't mean he or she isn't ever going to hit a backhand. In fact, the weak backhand will probably get more of a workout than the forehand during the match if the child's opponent is bright enough to figure out why he or she is constantly running around the backhand.

It would be pointless to try to list specific strategies for singles play because conditions vary from match to match, opponent to opponent, and even game to game. The best advice a parent, or anyone, can give a child is to go with his or her best shot whenever possible, to try to hit the open court, and to be flexible.

Strategy: Doubles Play

Doubles isn't necessarily twice as complicated as singles just because there are twice as many players involved. As a matter of fact, doubles play may be somewhat less demanding because each player has half as much court area to cover during a match. And since the responsibility for hitting the ball does not fall to the same player on every shot, there is often more time to prepare for those chances that do come a player's way. Obviously, this shot preparation factor does not apply to high level doubles matches in which rapid-fire net exchanges are commonplace, but in most recreation or family matches the pace is usually slow enough to allow plenty of preparation time.

Since the majority of doubles points are won off the volley, the main objective of the doubles team is to get to the net as quickly as possible. This means that the server should try to follow the serve to the net. The same strategy applies to the receiver.

Unfortunately, things don't always work out that way. If a doubles player becomes involved in a baseline rally, the other half of the partnership should remain at the net and keep his or her eyes on the opponents. You will be able to tell where your teammate's shot is headed by the reaction of the other players. Once you pick up the actual flight of the ball, be prepared to pounce on it if the return comes into your range.

If you happen to be the player involved in the baseline exchange while your partner is at the net, try to keep the ball deep and away from the opposing side's net player.

All doubles players should remember that a cooperative effort is necessary for success in a doubles match. They should, therefore, always try to operate as a tandem unit in which both members are equal partners.

A certain amount of communication should be a part of every doubles team's game plan. You will seldom if ever hear a singles player shout "Yours," when a well-placed lob sails over his head, during a match. That would, of course, be silly and pointless. In doubles, however, a certain amount of verbal communication is advisable. But the communications should, of necessity, be fairly brief, especially in the midst of a point. If, for example, both players are at the net and the opposition puts a lob down the middle, someone's going to have to make a fairly quick decision. This kind of exchange won't do:

"Hey it's a lob. Gee, I wasn't expecting that, were you?"

"No way. I was convinced they'd go to you. After all, you haven't hit a decent volley all day."

"I have too."

"Have not."

"Have too."

"Look, I'm not going to stand here and argue with you. Are you going to go after that lob or not?"

"*Me?* Why it is always me? It's about time *you* chased a lob."

"What are you talking about? I got the last one, remember?"

"Oh yeah. I forgot. Tell you what, let's flip for it."

"Good idea. Got a coin?"

Obviously, the lob under discussion landed on the court well before the impromptu summit conference ended, and likely as not, the opposing team has packed up and gone.

The point is that a simple "I've got it" or "Mine" or "You take it" or "Yours" will be sufficient.

On-court communication is important for a doubles team, but so is a bit of pre-match discussion. A good doubles partnership will decide in advance which player is going to be responsible for taking the shots down the middle. Normally, the player who is charged with this responsibility will play the side of the court that will keep his or her strong shot to the inside.

Besides being effective, this bit of preplanned strategy

132

will usually prevent a common feature of most recreational doubles matches: racquet collisions. It will also prevent the opposition from scoring easy points by hitting the ball down the middle.

Doubles has long been the most popular form of the game among recreational players, and it seems destined to continue as such since more and more tennis families are taking up tennis *en masse*. But whether your preference is for doubles or singles, you might consider inviting a few big-name pros into your living room to give you and your family some lessons in strategy.

How?

Simple. There's at least one, and often more than one, tennis match on the tube nearly every weekend. Just tune in and watch how the experts do it. I guarantee you'll pick up a few pointers.

10

The Emotional Game

Learning how to hold a tennis racquet, how to hit a tennis ball, and even how to think about where the ball should be directed is only part of the process by which a child becomes a tennis player.

There is another element of the game, and it cannot be ignored because it is the one that is most likely to make or break a young player. This crucial segment of tennis may be neatly tied up into a package and labeled "The Emotional Game." The package may be further marked with the warning "Fragile" and "Handle With Care."

Children who play tennis open this package every single time they step onto a tennis court. Their performances, no matter how basic or advanced, will be accompanied by a barrage of emotions. At one time or another they will experience joy, anger, frustration, and practically every other emotion listed in the catalogue of human feelings. And how children react to these feelings will depend a great deal on their individual emotional development. But every child can use some guidance in this area.

Though a child's practical tennis education is best left to

135

an instructor who is qualified to teach the mechanics of the game, the parent is clearly the child's most valuable ally when it comes to dealing with the emotions that are bound to surface while on the court.

But the parent can also become the child's enemy. This happens when the parent dismisses a child's emotional reactions to tennis, especially the ones that are negative, as a "phase" or, worse, as unimportant. The emotions a child must contend with on the tennis court are never unimportant.

Parents must understand that tennis, and every other sport, is a part of life. It is both foolish and unrealistic for parents to expect their children to develop two complete sets of emotions, one for sports and one for everything else in life. The child who is easily frustrated at school will probably be easily frustrated on the tennis court, and so on.

136

But don't just take my word for it. Listen to what Dr. Thomas Tutko, the co-founder of the Institute of Athletic Motivation and a psychology professor at San Jose State University, has to say about the correlation between sports and emotions. In his book *Sports Psyching*, Dr. Tutko offers the following observation:

"Friends get into fights over sports. Couples get divorced over sports. Rioters tear stadiums apart—and occasionally referees—over the outcome of a game. And all this is just over watching *other* people play.

"When we participate ourselves, these passions are felt more personally, but in the great scheme of things could be considered just as irrational. While playing what are supposed to be relaxing Sunday games, we behave in ways that would be regarded as signs of being mentally unbalanced if we did them off the field. We talk to ourselves. We curse inanimate objects. We throw things, become aggressive toward friends, and sometimes we even cheat (because the appearance of winning becomes more important than our self-respect). What pressures push us to these actions?

"Playing in a game is obviously not just a physical experience; it is a total personal experience. You don't leave your personality, habits, and attitudes behind when you walk onto the field. What you do there is recognized as 'physical activity,' *but the movement of every muscle involves you emotionally.* [Italics mine.] And it is the emotional charge—the feelings side of sport—that makes it so fascinating, exciting, and frustrating.

"This emotional charge comes from many directions. First, there are the *intrinsic* pressures to overcome the physical challenge that is a part of every game. Second, there are the *cultural* pressures from our society, which sets great store on superior athletic performance. Third, there are *personal* pressures, which derive from your own athletic experience and the ways you have learned to react to it."

This pretty well sums up why we react to sports on an emotional level, and it applies to children as well as adults.

I have already discussed a few of the ways in which parents may contribute to their children's enjoyment of the tennis experience, so now it's time to examine the other side of the coin: How to cope with some of the less than positive, and therefore potentially damaging, emotional reactions of the young tennis player.

Motivation

Once upon a time, there was a mule whose stubborn streak was positively legendary. In fact, this mule (we'll call it Jack) redefined the word stubborn. That trait, of course, didn't exactly thrill Jack's owner, Farmer Bill, who was really getting fed up with the lack of cooperation he was receiving.

But one day when Jack once again ignored his owner's threats, sweet talk, and pathetic pleas, and refused to budge, Farmer Bill was struck with a brilliant idea. He pulled a carrot out of his pocket (remember, he *was* a farmer); he found a piece of string and a long twig. Acting like a man possessed, the frustrated farmer quickly tied one end of the string to the carrot and the other end to the stick. Farmer Bill then took his strange invention and began applying it to Jack's hindquarters vigorously. This didn't go over real well with Jack, of course, but he still refused to move. Farmer Bill then noticed that the stubborn mule seemed to be trying to bite the carrot between swings.

Once again seized with inspiration, Farmer Bill climbed onto Jack's back and dangled the carrot a few inches in front of the recalcitrant beast's hungry eyes and salivating chops.

138

Jack figured, what the heck, it's worth taking one little step to get to that carrot, and he did just that. "Must've misjudged the distance," thought Jack upon realizing that the carrot was no closer than it had been before. So he took another step, and another, and still another. Still no carrot. Soon, the same stubbornness that made him refuse to move earlier took over and Jack refused to give up the carrot chase, futile though it was.

And that carrot *motivated* the mule all the way home. Which leads *us* right into a discussion of motivation as it applies to tennis, children, and parents.

Of course, I'm not suggesting that parents should dangle a carrot, not literally anyway, in front of children who are either reluctant to play tennis at all or are on the verge of giving up the game. I do, however, think that parents who would like to see their offspring take up the game or continue playing once they've started should make a non-forceful attempt to motivate their children in that direction.

We all need some sort of inducement to get us going and to keep us going. The basic human need of food, for example, is a terrific motivating factor for a person to seek a job. And once a job is secured, raises and promotions are used to motivate the worker to raise the level of his or her performance.

The parent, therefore, should try to find an effective, but figurative, carrot-on-a-stick that will lure the reluctant child onto the tennis court. The inducement chosen, however, must be a positive one. Force, threats, withholding food, or feigning nervous breakdowns that are intended to lay a massive guilt trip on the child won't do at all. Likewise, offers of great sums of money are to be avoided. Besides, one of the most effective motivational tools at a parent's disposal won't cost a cent.

Motivating by *example* just might inspire the child. Children react to their parents, so parental enthusiasm for tennis could very well be transmitted to the child.

If you have been frustrated in your efforts to get your child onto the court, examine what picture of a tennis player *you* present. If all the child sees is an angry, frustrated, or depressed father or mother who is constantly moaning or complaining about his or her tennis game, the child will probably conclude that tennis isn't a whole lot of fun.

But if you come home from a session at the court smiling and contented, the child just might figure, "Hey, if tennis is so much fun for old people, it's gotta be fun for kids."

Coaxing a reluctant child onto the court is only the beginning, however. Children are a lot smarter than Jack, the carrot-grubbing mule. They will not respond to tennis for very long unless they receive some gratification from their involvement.

Obviously, different children require different gratification. For some, consistent progress will keep them interested; for others, just having a good time will be enough. The latter will undoubtedly be playing for a long, long time because their gratification won't depend on their performance. That could change at any time though, and then they will be in the same

140

position as progress-oriented children. And that position is tenuous indeed.

The child who places all his or her emphasis on progress and performance and very little on sheer enjoyment will eventually reach a plateau where further progress is either slowed to an almost imperceptible crawl or ceases altogether. When that happens, the gratification disappears and so does the child's interest in playing tennis.

Of course, the parents of a child who simply falls head over heels in love with the game don't have to worry about providing motivation and gratification. My parents never did because that's exactly what happened to me. Initially, my sole reason for playing tennis was nothing more complicated or mysterious than a passion for anything and everything that had to do with the sport. But secondary motivations began to appear almost immediately.

Before I barely knew how to hold a tennis racquet properly, I made up my mind that someday I'd be the best tennis player in the world. That was one admittedly lofty motivation. I always wanted a career in sports, and tennis, though not especially lucrative at the time, seemed to be a good vehicle for getting one. Another motivational factor.

Still another was the discovery that tennis would fulfill my long-standing desire to travel, provided, of course, that I could improve enough to play on the international circuit.

There were other motviations, but even if none of them had been gratified (and most have been), I would still have had numero uno: my love of tennis.

It is beyond any parent's capability to instill a deep and abiding love of tennis in a child, and your child seems to be immune to the contagious enthusiasm you are trying to spread by example. What then? How do you motivate the child?

First of all, ask yourself *why* you want the child to play

tennis. Are you concerned because he or she doesn't seem to be interested in *anything*? Is it because the family doubles match needs a regular fourth? Is it because you feel that if tennis is good enough for you, it's certainly good enough for your son or daughter? (This question isn't as off-the-wall as it might seem. It is quite common for parents to either consciously or subconsciously want their life-style to be reinforced by their children.) Is it, heaven forbid, because you want your child to earn a million dollars playing tennis?

If your reason for wanting to motivate your child is a sensible one, you are well within your rights to attempt some direct action. Actually, even if your reasons are completely screwed up, you're within your rights to take direct action, but you will be wrong. Either way, your first step is to sit down with the child and find out why he or she is either disillusioned with tennis or not the least bit interested in giving it a try.

First, let's consider the case of a child who has never played tennis and doesn't seem particularly anxious to try it. The burden of opening the discussion automatically falls to you, the parent. I mean the child's probably not going to approach you and say, "Can we talk about why I hate tennis?" So you must get things rolling.

"Can we talk for a minute?"

"Sure thing, Parent."

"Good. Basically, I'd like to know why you seem to dislike tennis."

"I don't know. I just don't like it. I've already told you that about a million times."

"I know, but it just occurred to me that perhaps you have a more specific reason."

"Maybe. But I'd rather not say what it is."

Aha. Progress. Now we're getting somewhere. Go easy and don't blow it.

142

"Why not? Look, whatever it is you have against playing tennis certainly isn't going to upset me. I just want to know what it is."

"You'll laugh."

"No I won't. Promise."

"Okay. Here it is: I don't want to play tennis now or ever because I think it is the stupidest, silliest game on earth. I want to play baseball and basketball. Now those sports make sense."

"Why didn't you tell me this before?"

"I was afraid you'd get angry."

"Oh."

Well, now you know. The child thinks tennis is a stupid, silly game. You don't agree, of course, but arguing about it probably won't solve anything.

Look at it this way: You think golf (or football or hockey or skydiving or whatever) is a stupid, silly sport and no one's going to get you out onto a golf course (or football field, hockey rink, or into an airplane with a parachute strapped to your back, or whatever), right? Of course not. So you shouldn't try to get your child onto a tennis court. And don't tell the child that his or her opinion is stupid and silly. Children are people too, and they are entitled to hold opinions about what games they want or don't want to play.

End the conversation gracefully. Like this:

"If I'd known you felt that strongly about tennis, I wouldn't have bugged you about playing."

"Really?"

"Really. But if you happen to change your mind . . . ?"

"I know, there's always room for one more tennis player in this world."

"Right."

But if the child's reasoning goes something like "I'm afraid to play tennis because it looks so complicated that I'm sure I could never learn to play," the door's wide open for you to waltz right in and remove that fear.

Don't say, "Is that all? Why, that's the dumbest reason I ever heard for being afraid to play tennis." Try to be more tactful than that. It shouldn't be too difficult, because being less tactful is hard to imagine. Let the child know that you can understand how someone could be intimidated by a sport like tennis, but that millions of people learn how to play every year. Acknowledge the child's fear, but dismiss it gently and without ridicule. Be sure to tell the child that you certainly don't expect him to become a tennis whiz kid, that you just want him to have fun.

The same degree of understanding and encouragement is effective when dealing with the child who has played tennis for a while but whose interest is deteriorating rapidly.

"Hey, it's almost two o'clock, and you're not ready. Did you forget that the big match is today? You and I are taking on your dad and your brother this week."

"I really don't feel much like playing tennis today."

"You haven't felt like playing for a couple of weeks now. How come?"

"I'd rather not say."

Here we go again. Patience, Mother, patience.

"Why not?"

"I don't want to start anything."

"Don't worry, you won't. I just want to know what's been bothering you."

"Actually, I've been trying to figure out a way of telling you for a while now. I guess this is as good a time as any. I'm thinking of giving up tennis because it's kind of a hassle."

"What do you mean exactly?"

"Well, every time the family plays there's a lot of yelling and screaming and you and Dad always seem to get in a fight. That bothers me a lot."

144

"I guess you're right. We aren't exactly the Waltons of the tennis court, are we? Would you change your mind about playing if things changed?"

"Sure. It used to be fun when we first started playing, and I'd like for it to be that way again."

"Me too. Let's see what we can do about it."

Whether that particular problem can be worked out or not depends on the family involved, but recognizing that it exists is certainly a step in the right direction.

But suppose the child was thinking of quitting for a far different reason. Suppose she had said: "I really had a lot of fun playing tennis in the beginning, but lately all I do is get upset when I miss a shot. I've tried not to let it bother me, but I can't help it. Besides, what I'd really love to do is concentrate on my swimming. Swimming is always fun, and I think I have a pretty good chance of making the school team."

Unless you want a depressed daughter moping around the house, you'd better let her go. A happy swimmer is better than a disenchanted tennis player any day of the week.

Farmer Bill (remember him?) was faced with the problem of motivating a dumb animal, and he eventually succeeded. But parents who attempt to motivate their children are dealing with extremely sensitive and complex creatures, so success is never a sure thing. But it's certainly worth the effort.

Temperament and Sportsmanship

Though I've been known to throw my racquet once in a while and on at least one occasion I walked off the court in the middle of a match (to protest the tournament referee's refusal to remove a linesperson who had made a series of blatantly bad calls), I believe that I have always adhered to the essence of good sportsmanship: respect for my opponents.

I have, of course, gotten angry at the person on the other

side of the net on occasion, but I've never intentionally tried to hurt or embarrass an opponent. Nor have I ever refused to congratulate one who had beaten me.

But many people will say that's not good enough, that good sportsmanship goes beyond just respecting your opponent. And maybe they're right. But it's as good a place as any for parents to begin teaching their children about good sportsmanship. And parents *should* take an active role in shaping their children's behavior on the tennis court.

Tennis has a long and rich tradition of being a gentle sport—a "sissy" sport in the eyes of some—and an unwritten code of proper court behavior was established over the years. This code demanded that tennis players keep their emotions, and especially their anger, on the back burner. If a bad call was to be questioned at all, it had to be done with extreme politeness. Along the way, however, a few players violated the code often and loudly. These players were usually looked upon as talented cretins in a sport that put a huge premium on impeccable court deportment.

Then, as tennis began to offer vast sums of real money to the players instead of loving cups, silver trays, and tiny per diems, the code of proper behavior began to take more and more abuse. Some players, including Bob Hewitt of South Africa, Ion Tiriac of Rumania, Billie Jean King of Houghton Park and environs, and, of course, the center court jester himself, Ilie Nastase, were often accused of trying to turn the staid sport of tennis into something that was a cross between Ringling Brothers and Barnum & Bailey and Big Time Wrestling.

The folks who leveled these accusations at any player who showed a tendency to be demonstrative during play usually pointed to Stan Smith, Arthur Ashe, and Chris Evert as perfect examples of how every tennis player should behave.

I strongly disagree.

146

But before you jump to the completely erroneous conclusion that I am advocating that you groom your child to be a racquet-throwing, obscenity-spewing anarchist on the tennis court, let me explain.

Professional tennis players are under a tremendous amount of pressure while they're playing, and some of us react to certain situations in ways that might take us out of the running for the "Perfect Little Lady or Gentleman Tennis Player" award. For me, personally, a display of anger is a psychological safety valve of sorts. That doesn't mean I step onto the court looking for an opportunity to fly off the handle, though. My anger on the court is never contrived, and I certainly don't enjoy getting angry. But I'm an extremely intense person who, unfortunately, also has a fairly low boiling point and sometimes I have to let off some steam.

Over the years I have tried many, many times to learn to control my emotions on the court, or at least the outward signs of them, and to some degree I've succeeded. But there are still times when something sets me off (and it's usually me I'm angry at), and I fling the ol' racquet and start yelling. On such occasions, my mind is saying, "Shut up, Billie. You're making a fool of yourself again," but I can't help it.

I have always been this way, and I probably always will be. And do you know why? Because I am an intense, high-strung, deeply feeling, non-perfect human being, that's why.

They say that confession is good for the soul, and that is probably true. But my confession of the obvious just makes it that much more difficult for me to give advice on how to handle your child's tennis court behavior. Still, I'm going to try. But first, I want to set your mind at ease about your child being influenced by the behavior of a temperamental pro tennis player.

A lot of kids look up to professional athletes, of course, and many impressionable youngsters are prompted to imitate whichever athlete they happen to admire. Your concern over your child's admiration of, say, Ilie Nastase is therefore quite legitimate. But the problem may not be nearly as bad as you might suspect. If you enjoy a good rapport with your child, and I'm assuming you do, *you* are going to have a greater effect on your child's behavior than a thousand Nastases.

Sit down and talk to the child about which of Nastase's qualities he finds so appealing. The child might very well surprise you by saying that Nastase is an amazingly talented

148

player (which is true), but that sometimes he acts a little crazy. Of course the child might say, "I think it's neat when he starts running around yelling at everybody." If that happens, explain that although you admire Nastase's ability, you think his antics are distasteful because they divert attention from his tennis skills, and that's a real shame.

Letting your child know how you feel about something will often affect the way he or she feels about it. Telling the child *what* to feel, however, is risky and may lead to a natural rebellion.

But what do you do if your child begins to demonstrate certain negative behavior patterns on the court? Do you brisky apply a sheathed tennis racquet to the young player's backside? Do you forbid him to play tennis until he vows to stop throwing the racquet and leaving teeth marks on the net tape? Or do you look the other way and try to pretend he belongs to someone else?

That was precisely the problem my own parents faced when I was a young player. My court behavior was exemplary most of the time, but I must admit I did have my moments. Naturally, my mother and father weren't exactly thrilled by my occasional outbursts, and they did everything they could to bring them to a screeching halt—but without much success. I didn't ignore their threats or pleadings; it's just that I couldn't contain my feelings all the time.

Because of my, shall we say, expertise in this area, I would advise parents of somewhat uninhibited young tennis players not to push the panic button at the first sign of temperament. Don't ignore it, but be careful not to go overboard either. Tailor your reaction to your child's particular transgression. If the child develops the habit of physically assaulting his or her opponent, he or she should be removed from the court, pronto. But throwing a racquet against the fence is a lot different than throwing it at the person on the other side of the net.

If the child occasionally does the former but never the latter, the first thing you should do is arrange a parent/child conference. Find out why the kid finds it necessary to throw his or her racquet. A typical answer:

"Cuz I get so mad I can't see straight when I miss an easy shot. I don't mean to throw my racquet. It just happens."

"Does it help?"

"No. Usually it just makes me even madder."

"Then what happens? Do you miss even more shots?"

"Yeah. How did you know that?"

"Well, sometimes getting angry can make you forget what you're supposed to do and that makes things worse. And the worse they get, the madder you get, and so on."

"So what am I supposed to do?"

"I think the first thing is to stop throwing your racquet, because it looks pretty ridiculous. I would also suggest that you try to control your anger. Everybody misses easy shots once in a while, but if it gets you mad, try to remember that you might miss another one just because you're angry. It won't be easy but you should give it a try."

"I will."

Notice that the parent explained that anger on the court can work against a player. There's certainly no doubt about that. I've often had a match slip from my grasp because I was so enraged that I was unable to concentrate. But anger can also be constructive if the player is able to channel it properly, though that doesn't happen very often.

The parent also showed a lot of wisdom by not telling the child to refrain from getting angry while playing tennis. The parent recognized that feelings and emotions cannot be legislated and made no attempt to do so. If children get angry or

150

frustrated on the tennis court, it's because they are responding to a particular situation. Unless the situation is changed, or the children learn to control the resultant anger, they will get mad simply because that's just the way they are.

In this case the anger was caused by a situation—missing easy shots—that will remain constant as long as the child continues to play tennis. But by advising the child to try to control or redirect that anger, the parent said exactly the right thing.

Although it is ridiculous for parents to try to legislate their children's feelings and emotions, distasteful tennis court behavior that results from these feelings can and should be dealt with quickly and firmly. But parents should allow a little leeway in this area. A display of emotion, positive or negative, is nothing to get upset about, as long as it's kept within reason. After all, children are human beings too.

Competition and Winning

These aspects of tennis are extremely difficult for me to discuss objectively because of my perception of the subject matter. I mean, after almost twenty-five years of busting my gut to win tennis matches, it would be pretty hypocritical of me to say winning isn't really all that important. So I'm not going to say that. Winning is extremely important to me, and it always has been.

I possess a powerful aversion to losing in anything I do, but that doesn't mean I'm a stranger to losing. Actually, I know all about it. During my first year or so of tournament competition I lost a lot of tennis matches, and I lost them big! For a while there, if I lost love-and-one, it was a *good* day.

I didn't particularly like losing, but since my ultimate goal was to be Number One someday, I knew that I had to learn to lose before I could become a winner. Still, it really used to tear me apart to work so hard to win a match and then not be able to quite pull it off.

Now if you're beginning to get the impression that I'm unaware of all the well-formulated and widely circulated arguments about how winning in sports is being grossly over-emphasized and is placing an unnecessary burden on young children, you're wrong. I have read the arguments that hold that view, and I've also talked to several of the people who've written them. And I agree with them . . . up to a point. The problem is I'm not entirely sure where that "point" is.

Obviously, winning is very, very important to a professional athlete. If the athlete is part of a team, he or she is paid to win, while in the individual sports an athlete's income is directly dependent on performance (i.e., winning); the more they win, the more they earn. This, however, doesn't mean that money is the sole motivational factor that makes pro athletes want to win. Sure, there are those in every sport who are in it only for the money, but the majority of professional athletes are simply people who are fortunate enough to be doing something they love and getting paid for it. Like me, for example.

I have spent the past decade or so playing tennis for increasingly larger prize money purses, but, and this is a very important but, I spent a dozen years before that playing for trophies, small expense allowances, and an occasional under-the-table payment. And during those dozen years there was never any guarantee that tennis would one day offer players such as myself the opportunity to make an extremely good living from the sport.

I played tennis because I loved the game, and my personal pride prompted me to bust my gut to win every time I stepped onto a court. But I wasn't alone, not by a long shot. Over the years, literally thousands of athletes endured hardships and

152

made sacrifices to play amateur tennis for exactly those same reasons.

Because I had long believed that athletes should have the opportunity to earn a living playing sports, no one was happier than I was when the tennis establishment finally, and officially, recognized professionalism. But the money that suddenly became available certainly didn't affect my desire to win tennis matches, nor did it affect the intense competitive spirit that characterized the women's tour during the amateur years. All the money did was make the life of a tennis player easier and focus more attention on the sport.

And whether you're talking about tennis or baseball, bowling or basketball, golf or football, the fact remains that winning, for whatever reason, is extremely important to the person who earns his or her living playing the game. And rightfully so. But the overwhelming majority of eight-year-old children are not professional athletes. What about them? How large a role should competition and winning play in their lives?

I think that a good deal of that particular decision should be left up to the child. Unfortunately, however, many children never get a chance to make that decision because some adult has already made it for them. Sometimes the adult is the child's parent, sometimes it is the adult-organized-and-operated children's sports system (Little League baseball, Pee Wee football, junior tennis tournaments, etc.), and sometimes it's a combination of the parent, the system, and the coach.

The child who enters the world of organized athletic competition is almost inevitably confronted by a dazzling array of statistics, standings, and other "major league" influences he doesn't need and may not want.

I'm not totally against all organized athletic competition for children, but I do think it's a grave mistake when a system or a coach imposes a philosophy of winning on a child. And that, of course, is a common feature of organized sports programs for youngsters. But, I also think it's a mistake for a parent or a coach to tell a child that competition and winning aren't important at all.

Competition and winning are basic features in our society and our lives. School is a very real form of competition where the winners get high marks, and we make our children go to school and reward them with praise when they earn (win) those high marks. Why do parents shower their children with praise for earning (winning) high marks? Because the high marks are supposed to be indicative of an ability to learn, and an ability to learn will someday land many children in a higher form of competition called college. But whether they go on to this higher form of competition or not, all children will someday find themselves in the midst of the ultimate competition: finding a job and earning a living.

In view of this, it strikes me as somewhat paradoxical when someone, and especially someone who has a hard-won college degree, says that sports competition for children is harmful.

"Sports are supposed to be fun for children," they say, and I couldn't agree more. "But," they continue, "an emphasis on competition and winning can only dilute the child's fun."

I'll go along with the latter part of that statement . . . if the emphasis on winning is determined by someone other than the child. But the competition part? No way.

It's as impossible to separate competition from sports as it is to separate sports from life. Sport *is* competition. A jogger on a morning run is engaged in competition. To be sure, there is no opponent, no timekeeper, and no wildly cheering crowd waiting for him or her to cross the finish line. In fact there may not even be a finish line. But there is competition: with oneself. And we are usually the most challenging opponent we will ever face.

154

By now you may be wondering what specific words of advice I'm going to offer regarding the obviously complex problem of winning, competition, and the young tennis player. You may even be afraid that I'm going to advocate turning every child into a wild-eyed, win-at-all-costs fanatic. Well, you can relax.

I've already mentioned that I think children should be allowed to decide just how important winning is for *them*, but you can and should provide your children with some input about the relative importance of winning and losing.

For instance, you should let them know that winning, contrary to the well-known slogan or battle cry, *isn't* everything. Losing a tennis match, or any athletic contest, certainly doesn't carry with it an irrevocable sentence that is imposed upon the loser to spend the rest of his or her days in a damp, black pit as implied by the winning-is-the-whole-enchilada line.

Tell your child that he shouldn't ever be afraid of losing, but that he shouldn't be afraid of *winning* either. Surprisingly, a lot of children (and adults) are afraid to win. They can't stand the pain of trying to win and then losing, so they gradually build up a subconscious will to fail. And pretty soon they *can't* win.

This particular phenomenon is not unknown at the highest levels of tennis competition. Often young, unknown players will have someone like Chris Evert or Jimmy Connors on the ropes when suddenly the unknowns wake up and say, "This isn't right. I was supposed to get trampled in this match, but here I am up four-love in the final set. Something's wrong."

And, of course, the programed losers usually end up losing the next six games and the match just because they found themselves in a position of being on the verge of winning and it scared them.

Finally, you should tell your child winning can be something different for each person. For some, it may mean winning every game in a match; for others it may mean just doing the best they possibly can and finishing the match. The latter folks will always be winners, regardless of what the score says.

But whatever emphasis your child places on winning in tennis be sure to let him know that it's not going to affect how you feel about him.

And once your child is in competition, carefully observe how he reacts to losses. If he places a lot of emphasis on winning score-wise and losing causes him to become mildly depressed for brief periods of time, that's perfectly normal. Commiserate with him, but try not to be overly sympathetic or you'll run the risk of reinforcing losing by the attention you give.

If, however, the child plunges into a deep and extended funk after every loss on the tennis court, you should encourage

156

him to think through the situation carefully. If he is unable to alter his reactions to losing, but is unwilling to drop tennis for another sport, you might try tacking the following words to his bedroom door:

"Winning and losing in sports are but a few transitory moments in the greater scheme of things. Dwelling on either of them is not a particularly good idea, especially when you could be watching 'Star Trek' reruns instead."

I don't know who said that, but it makes sense to me.

II

So Your Child Wants

to Be a Pro?

Ninety-nine percent of the children who take up tennis will never earn a living from the sport, and so far this book has been aimed at them and their parents. But the one percent who *will* someday make it to the pro ranks should not be ignored.

As tennis' popularity continues to grow, and I think it will, more and more children are going to set their sights on a career as a professional tennis player and a few of them will succeed. It's entirely possible that your child could be among them, so you'd better be prepared. If it does happen, both you and your child will be facing many monumental obstacles that parents of those children who are content to play tennis purely recreationally will never meet.

Here then are a few guidelines for you to follow when your child suddenly announces that he or she is going to become a professional tennis player.

First of all, let me offer my congratulations to both the potential pro and to you, the parent of the potential pro. Tennis is an honorable profession and one that you may be proud your child has chosen. I'm sure you'll agree that it's certainly better than having your son or daughter aspiring to become a cat burglar or a Mafia hit-man, and it beats the heck out of unemployment.

But although a career in tennis, or any other professional sport, can be rewarding, both personally and financially, it is a difficult, highly pressurized, and often short-lived undertaking. Because of these and other reasons, many parents will try to discourage a child right from the start.

"A professional tennis player, huh? That's pretty funny."

"Why?"

"Oh, don't be ridiculous. There are millions of tennis players around and how many of them make it to the pros? Well, I'll tell you how many. A couple of hundred at the most. A couple of hundred out of all those millions and millions."

"I know it won't be easy, but . . ."

"Won't be *easy*? Can't be done is more like it. Look, it's never going to happen, so why don't you just have a little fun with tennis and forget about the big time. Otherwise, you'll be letting yourself in for a big disappointment. Besides, why can't you just aim for a career as a nurse like little girls did when I was your age?"

At least part of what the parent said makes good sense. There *are* millions of tennis players around and only a very few of them ever play professionally. But the way in which the parent presented this information to the child (who probably was aware of it anyway) could have been handled a lot better.

Maybe the parent was motivated by a very real concern for the child, but that's no justification for shooting down the kid's dream, whether that dream is realistic or not.

Now let's give the child another dream and see how the parent reacts.

"Mom, I've decided that I want to be a brain surgeon someday."

"A brain surgeon, huh? That's fine. But you realize, of course, that it's not going to be easy. People don't just wake up one morning and know how to operate on brains. They have to work for it and work hard. It takes years and years of study."

"Well, I know my grades haven't been too hot lately, but starting right now I'm going to work hard at school."

"That's certainly a good start. Just remember to take it one step at a time. If you really want to become a brain surgeon, then go for it. I'll be right here to help you in whatever way I possibly can."

"Thanks, Mom."

Notice that the parent didn't say, "Forget about being a brain surgeon, because you're too dumb to be a tree surgeon." Instead, she encouraged the child. And that's exactly how you should react to your child's ambitions toward becoming a professional tennis player.

But try not to go overboard. Controlled enthusiasm is the best way to handle it at first. Too much enthusiasm and unconditional encouragement could lead to trouble later on.

The average child probably changes career objectives a couple of times a week, and a parent who overacts in a "positive" manner may unwittingly place an enormous psychological burden on the child's shoulders. The parent who greets a child's announced intentions of becoming a pro tennis player by saying, "Fantastic! Having a professional athlete in the family will make my drab, dull life complete," probably thinks that's what the child wants to hear. And maybe the youngster does, at that moment. But what about two days or two weeks or two months from then when the child decides he wants to be a pharmacist instead of a tennis player?

160

How can he face the parent and say, "Sorry, but I'm afraid I'm going to have to let you down and leave you with an incomplete life after all. Unless, of course, you feel the same way about having a pharmacist in the family."

Obviously, burdening the child with a potentially disastrous load of guilt is not good, but even the most gentle insinuation that he might not have the ability to reach the top is even worse.

When I was sixteen years old, two women's tennis champions, Alice Marble and Maureen Connolly, told me that I'd never make it to the top, and I was pretty well devastated by the two experiences. I never really discovered the reasons behind their remarks, which, by the way, were delivered less than pleasantly, and that's always bothered me. Perhaps they were using reverse psychology to spur me on. In any event, it took me a long time to recover from the dual shock. But because my particular vision for myself was too strong to be broken, I came through it alright.

I'm not trying to set myself up as some sort of tower of strength and intestinal fortitude, but I believe that many children, and perhaps most children, would have crumpled in a similar situation.

Never ever tell your child that he or she isn't good enough to entertain thoughts of a professional tennis career. If they aren't they'll find out for themselves. And don't worry, they'll be able to handle whatever degree of disappointment accompanies that discovery.

There is, however, one thing you can tell children who are anxious to join the international tennis circuit. You can tell them that they have to finish elementary school first. In fact, you should insist on it. Even tennis players need an education in something besides hitting tennis balls.

But if the child's desire to play professionally is undiluted by the passage of time, you will have to think about supplementing the formal education with an advanced course in tennis somewhere along the line. Progress in tennis is usually quite rapid at first, but as a player's skill level gets better and better, progress slows down and eventually comes to a halt. When that happens, further progress will require the services of a qualified tennis coach. Coaching helps refine different aspects of a fundamentally strong game.

Though I spent five or six years as a pupil of Clyde Walker, there came a time when I needed some help that he, good as he was, wasn't able to provide. Clyde recognized that he'd taken me as far as he could, and he was quite insistent that I take advantage of an opportunity to work with Alice Marble, one of the all-time great tennis players. Of course, Alice and I had a little falling out eventually, but before that happened my parents used to drive me up to her house every weekend, and we'd work out on a private court nearby. My game advanced under Alice's instruction, but I also learned a great deal about what it was like to be a champion from her.

I was very fortunate to have someone of Alice Marble's stature as a coach, but a good tennis coach, like a good group instructor, doesn't necessarily have to have been a champion. But the tennis coach you choose for your child *will* have to be an astute student of the game to be effective, so choose carefully.

Coaching is the tennis education's equivalent of college, but tournament competition is the graduate school and thesis all rolled into one. The child who is serious about a pro career will require competition and lots of it.

I lucked out in this area of my tennis development because I happened to live in the land of freeways and sun-bleached smog and a lot of tennis activity. I was able to participate in a juniors tournament practically every single week.

Junior tournaments are amateur events that are open to all players who are under eighteen years of age, though some major events like the U.S. Open and Wimbledon have a twenty-one-and-under bracket. Generally, however, there are five age-group divisions within each junior tournament. They are: ten-and-under, twelve-and-under, fourteen-and-under, sixteen-and-under, and, of course, eighteen-and-under. These tournaments are held all over the country, and there are probably a couple of them staged near where you live every year. Your child should play in as many of these events as possible, and there's the rub.

If you don't happen to reside in an area where junior tournaments are available on a regular basis, some travel will be required. This, of course, can put a tremendous strain on your finances.

Many areas do have civic groups and tennis associations that offer financial assistance to talented juniors, and many people who live near tournament sites graciously open their homes to visiting out-of-town players. But the sad fact remains that there is never enough money to go around.

Unless a parent is independently wealthy, or a child is deemed worthy of receiving an assist from the local junior tennis association, the child's exposure to tournament play will be severely limited and that is as unfortunate as it is unavoidable. But I can't give you any easy answers to this problem. If you're willing to go into hock to finance your child's tennis career, that's your decision. But if you do, don't be disappointed if the child bails out of tennis somewhere along the line. Remember: The odds against a child making it to the

163

pros are monumental, and the world is full of supremely talented ex-juniors who never made it.

I hope your child succeeds.